# Too Precious for Earth

# Too Precious for Earth

Amy C. Maddocks

Est. R '06
BookWise
publishing

Too Precious for Earth



BookWise Publishing
P. O. Box 712137
Salt Lake City, UT 84171
www.bookwise.com

www.amymaddocks.com

Cover design: Brian Hailes, Salt Lake City, Utah
www.hailesart.com
Author photo: Jessica Smith
www.jessicasphoto.com
ISBN: 978-1-60645-025-3
10 9 8 7 6 5 4 3 2 1
First Printing

# Dedication

*To Connor*
*who leads for us the way to heaven*
*through our good works and charity*
*and is always a shining radiance of hope*
*during my gloomiest of days;*
*and to my family and friends*
*who put up with my silliness*
*and still love me unconditionally.*

*What we have once enjoyed we can never lose.*
*All that we love deeply becomes a part of us.*

- Helen Keller -

## CHAPTER ONE

# REALIZATIONS

I sat down on my bed, exhausted after another long day of emptiness. What to do now? I picked up the journal I bought a few nights previously, toying with the cover. On it was a picture of Christ, holding a baby boy and helping a young girl over some treacherous rocks. I hadn't known why this particular cover attracted my attention at the time. Now I understood why. It held more meaning for me than I could have ever thought possible. Looking at the picture, I felt a sudden surge of anger wash over me, and I threw it on my bed. *Another time,* I thought to myself.

But then I realized all I had was time—a whole lot of worthless, useless, unwanted time. So I picked the journal back up again, opened it to the first page, and let my eyes wander while my fingers caressed the paper.

On the first page was a pre printed title, "Journal." Underneath this I wrote, "For Connor." I felt it was appropriate. I turned the page and wrote the date, January 12, 2007. I have never been one to keep a journal. I have tried and failed many times over the course of my lifetime. But this time was different; this time it was for Connor, my son.

It felt weird thinking the words, *my son*. For over sixteen years I had wanted another child. My daughter, Alyssa, (whom we also call Lys) brought me such joy as a mother, that I always knew I wanted more children. I grew up with five siblings, and I thought six was the perfect number for a family. When asked what I wanted to be when I grew up, my answer was always the same: a mommy and a teacher. But for sixteen years after my daughter was born, I had been told I could not have more children.

My daughter was born nine weeks premature and my recovery from her delivery was very difficult. It took me many years of heartache to come to terms with the fact that I would only have one child. I had made it through all of the rude comments, like, "Be thankful you have at least one child," or the more popular, "I guess God only meant for you to have one child." Good grief. As if I wasn't eternally grateful for my daughter? She is a light in my life—who wouldn't want more of that? So I carefully dodged the uncouth remarks and questions about my lack of children.

Then I realized I might actually be pregnant again. It was in August of 2006 and I was on my way to Park City, Utah with my mother, sister, and daughter. We were spending a few days together shopping for school clothes. My daughter and sister are close to the same age, and they have always been very good friends. So we thought we'd go somewhere fun and hit the factory outlet stores while we were at it.

We live in northern Utah, and Park City is almost a two-hour drive. I had been noticing for a few weeks that I got very nauseous whenever I rode in a car, so I was expecting it. I had my garbage bucket and extra bags ready just in case. Sure enough, I fought throwing up the entire drive. We made it to the hotel, and I just didn't feel right. I lay down on the bed and tried to relax.

After about an hour, the girls were itching to go shopping, so I dragged myself off the bed and agreed to go. My mom was concerned because I am usually the life of the party. I have always been a believer that attitude is a little thing which makes a big difference. I am a school teacher, and even in my classroom, I try to teach my students how attitude can change their lives. So when I couldn't snap out of my icky mood, Mom started to worry. She tried convincing me to stay at the hotel while they went out, but my daughter was having none of that. I convinced them it was nothing and forced myself to be perky.

It worked for a while, and we got a lot of shopping done in a short amount of time—a talent of mine. But eventually, the feelings of "just not quite rightness" got the best of me and we went back to our room. I crashed for the night and slept like a rock. I am usually a light sleeper, but I zonked until morning came. That day I felt so much better—I just couldn't put my finger on why I was having these weird episodes. I finally attributed it to the blood-thinners I was taking (they made me feel different—never truly myself), and had a great time in Park City.

Later that evening, we returned to our hotel and freshened up for dinner. As I was doing my make-up in the mirror, a funny thought crossed my mind. I said it aloud, "Hey guys, maybe I'm puking because I'm pregnant!" We all laughed in unison.

My daughter said, "That's not funny, Mom," and gave me one of her 'serious' looks. Alyssa has never been keen on me having another child. When she hit her precocious teenager years, she decided she really enjoyed being an only child. She fully admits she's terribly spoiled. But then again, she's worth it.

After we all got a good laugh, and I assured Alyssa I could not possibly be pregnant, we went to a great restaurant and relaxed for the evening. However, something in the back of my mind kept nagging at me. I couldn't shake the feeling something was different. I kept arguing with myself that it truly wasn't possible for me to conceive.

But my mind was also playing tricks on me. I had been taking birth control pills for years, but only because I had Poly-cystic Ovarian Syndrome (PCOS) and it helped regulate the hormonal imbalance I dealt with. However, two months previously, I had stopped taking the pills because I was hospitalized with blood clots. The doctors still don't know how I got them. But the clots started in my leg and went to my lungs, so I ended up in the hospital for seven glorious days.

Because I could no longer take birth control pills, which cause blood clots, my hubby, Chas, and I talked about another form of birth control. We knew the chances of me getting pregnant were slim to none, but regardless, we looked into other options just in case. I was too out-of-shape to consider having another child at this point. Plus, we were in the middle of a nasty custody battle over my four step-children. Finances were extremely tight, and we knew we shouldn't be taking any chances—even if they were slim. Nevertheless, we didn't get around to using another form of birth control, thinking we were safe because I really couldn't conceive.

So I started going through my mind. *When was the last time I had felt normal and had my period?* I realized it had been a couple of months. Still, I had come to terms that I couldn't have any more children, so this just wasn't a possibility. I put the thought out of my head and made a decision to get a test done the following week—just in case. The rest of the trip was great—except the ride home. That Monday I went to my doctor's office to request a pregnancy test. I told my husband what I was doing. He didn't seem overly concerned. I figured I needed to know one way or the other and I wanted to be sure. I was taking blood-thinners and that couldn't be good for a fetus.

*As human beings, our greatness lies*
*not so much in being able to remake the world*
*as in being able to remake ourselves.*

- Mahatma Gandhi -

## CHAPTER TWO

# ARE YOU SURE?

"It's positive," said the nurse.

"What exactly do you mean by 'positive?'" I asked her. "Is that pregnant or not?"

"You're pregnant, Mrs. Maddocks."

*Was I hearing her correctly?*

I must have, because her next comment was, "Is this a good thing?"

"Um, are you sure?" I was in shock.

*Was this happening to me? Could it actually be true—or was this a dream?* She told me again that I was pregnant.

"Mrs. Maddocks, is this a good thing?" the nurse asked once more. I must have looked distraught, because she seemed concerned. Then I realized tears were in my eyes. She didn't know if they were tears of joy or pain.

"I, um, yes, I mean . . . I just don't know what to think. I haven't been able to conceive for seventeen years. I have PCOS and I'm not supposed to be able to have any more children. I just don't know what to think right now."

I was sitting on a bench a few feet away from her and I

realized everybody in that room had heard our conversation. People looked at me with both wonder and amusement—as if they had been in my exact situation before. They couldn't possibly know what I was experiencing. They were all pregnant and had a few kids running around them.

I made a huge effort to compose myself and tried to stand up. It didn't work. I immediately became dizzy and only made it halfway up before I had to sit again. The nurse came closer to me and asked if I was okay.

"I'm fine," I told her. "I just need to focus for a minute."

She got me a cup of water and came back to talk to me. I knew I was going to be crying uncontrollably at any moment and I had to get out of there fast.

I composed myself as best I could. The nurse told me to make an appointment with the front desk for the next one available. I thought that was odd, but by the time I made it to the front desk, she had beaten me to it with strict instructions from my doctor. I was to be seen the very next day no matter what the time. I talked to her about the different medications I was on and she advised me to stop taking the blood-thinners and talk to the doctor the next day.

I left the office in a daze. I felt like I was in a movie where the actress just received some shocking news and the camera is focused on her while she processes things. Her actions are slow and deliberate. She walks with precision to her car, fumbles with her keys, opens the car door and sits down. Staring at the steering wheel, she tries to focus on the task at hand, but can't seem to stop the tears. This was me—living a Hollywood moment. Except . . . I was pregnant! Unless the doctor's office was wrong, which was unlikely, a miracle had happened!

I needed to tell my husband. I was supposed to meet him at a plumbing supply store to order some parts for our sprinkler system. But I wanted to tell him in private. He had five children already—he was finished having kids. How was he going to take the news? I was worried. I decided to say they didn't have the results yet and tell him when we got home. I couldn't believe I was prepared basically to lie to my sweetheart, but I just couldn't tell him at the plumbing supply store.

I picked up my cell phone and dialed his number.

"Hi honey. I'm just leaving the doctor's office and I'll be there in five minutes," I told him.

Chas hesitated, then said, "So, what did the doctor say?"

"They did the test but I had to leave before I got the results so they are going to call later with them." I don't believe in dishonesty. But I just had to wait to tell him.

"Okay, but I thought those tests were pretty quick. Oh well, we'll find out then. See you soon," he said.

We said our goodbyes and I continued on my way through traffic.

I met him at the store a few minutes later and went through the motions of pretending everything was just the same as before. We did what we needed to do and I kissed him goodbye as we left in separate cars for the ride home. That was one of the longest ten minutes of my life. I kept going through my mind how I was going to tell him. I was so worried he was going to be angry with me. But then I kept telling myself he was a good man, an excellent father, and a wonderful husband. He would be okay with this—or would he?

*There is no life—no life without its hunger;*
*Each restless heart beats so imperfectly;*
*But when you come and I am filled with wonder,*
*Sometimes, I think I glimpse eternity.*

- Lyrics from "You Raise Me Up"

as sung by Josh Groban -

## CHAPTER THREE

# MIRACLE NUMBER TWO

We got home and went into the house. I hadn't made it three steps past the threshold before I started crying. Deep inside myself I was so worried Chas would be mad at me.

The year before we married, he talked all the time of how precious it would be to have children with me. I warned him it was impossible, and when we married, he changed his tune. He denied he had ever talked of having more kids. I think it was his way of letting me know it was "okay" that I wasn't able to have more children, but I always thought he truly didn't want any more. He had five girls from a previous marriage. One was an adult and married, but four were still young. Now, add up child support and do the math—it gets *very* expensive.

We had joint custody of his kids, but children are a lot more expensive when they live away from you. They lived with us the first year-and-a-half of our marriage, so we knew how much it really cost to take care of a large family. Since that time, we have been in and out of court trying to arrange things so the kids could come and live with us—something the children wanted as well—but it's very hard and extremely expensive to take that course of action. However, we felt like Chas's ex-wife was trying to get revenge for our trying to get full custody of the kids, so we had to pay her a lot more money than it actually cost to take care of them. We realized it was not only her way of getting back at us, but to also break us financially so we couldn't afford to continue our pursuit of full custody.

We were trying our best to take care of them financially when they were here *and* pay their mother the full amount of support at the same time. With a new baby, the cost of living magically goes up. So, yeah, having another child had to be the *last* thing on his priority list.

Pulling myself back to the present, I blurted out, "I'm pregnant. I don't know what to do. I know I told you I didn't know yet, but I just couldn't tell you at the plumbing store. It just didn't seem right. And with those other people around, I had to keep pretending until I was alone with you. I would have told you if we had driven together, but we didn't. So I didn't tell you and now I am and I just don't know what we're going to do. I know it's bad timing, but . . ."

"Amy, slow down. Stop crying. Why are you so upset?"

Could this be happening? I was standing there in more shock than I was when they told me I was pregnant. I couldn't understand why he wasn't upset. Maybe he hadn't really heard me?

Chas took me in his arms and held me. I sometimes feel

there is no safer place than in the comfort of my husband's arms. At six-foot-three and two-hundred-and-fifty pounds, he makes for a very intimidatinging-looking fellow. But that's also one of the many things I love about him. He looks like he could tear you to pieces in two breaths, but really he's a great big teddy bear. He truly has a heart of gold. And as I stood there in his arms, sobbing, he gently said to me, "We'll just say this is miracle number two."

My heart stopped beating in that moment. Chas was referring to my daughter from a previous marriage. She was born weighing at a whopping three pounds. She was in the hospital for a month after she was born and came home with all sorts of medications and machines hooked up to her in case she stopped breathing or her heart stopped beating. She truly was a miracle.

"Oh, Chas, are you serious? You aren't mad?"

"Are you kidding? Honey, if we are meant to have a child, then we will find a way to make it work. Obviously this was meant to be. You're not supposed to be able to even get pregnant. Look at what an absolute miracle this is!"

Now that I knew Chas was okay with the situation, I wanted to shout it out to the world. I told him so, but then in my mind, things turned sour. He felt we should keep this to ourselves until everything looked okay with the doctor. He asked me how things went at the doctor's office and I told him everything. He seemed concerned that they wanted to see me right away, but we decided not to worry about things until we had to.

We sat on the couch together and started talking about

what we were going to do. Curiously, one of our first thoughts was, *'How did this happen?'* Funny how that pops into your head—as if we didn't know. Nevertheless, we wanted to try and figure out when. I could technically be two months along, because the last time I had my period had been during my hospital stay from the blood clots. We suddenly realized that was when I had stopped taking birth control.

The more we got to talking about it, the more we realized what a true miracle this baby was. Chas had been taking a form of chemotherapy to help control a skin condition. He had been using a medication called Methotrexate, which lowers sperm counts so drastically that it's next to impossible to conceive while taking it. Then we also started to worry about all the medications I had been on.

We went to bed that night so apprehensive that neither of us could sleep. I had no idea at the time what a whirl-wind of events was about to befall us.

*"I can only imagine*
*what it will be like,*
*when I walk by your side.*
*I can only imagine,*
*what my eyes will see*
*when your face*
*is before me.*
*I can only imagine."*

- Song lyrics to "I Can Only Imagine"

as sung by Mercy Me -

## CHAPTER FOUR

# BIG SISTER

I teach language arts to eleven and twelve year-olds. It was so hard the next day to get through teaching groups of hyperactive prepubescent teenagers. I just wanted the day to end so I could get to the doctor's office and find out if my baby was going to be okay. I also desperately wanted to tell everyone. I knew it was unwise and Chas made me promise not to tell anyone until we had talked to the doctor and received some advice. So I kept to myself, even so much as to avoid the faculty room in case I spilled the news.

When we arrived at the doctor's office that afternoon, it was so wonderful to be treated like a queen. The nurses acted as though I was the most important person to them right at that moment. I felt like I was suddenly part of a club that only special people had the privilege of being in.

When I first started seeing Dr. Nordell ten years before, I felt uncomfortable at his office because it seemed like everybody was pregnant. However, as I got to know the nurses and staff, pretty soon I felt like I was normal. Yet, there was always something different about me—as if I had some aura around me that yelled to other women that I could not have children.

It had taken me years of heartache and help from Dr. Nordell to be okay with the fact that I couldn't have more children. But he had been with me through all the hard times and I trusted him. This time I was being seen in his office for something different. Something that put me in that prestigious club that I had never belonged to.

As I could have guessed, Dr. Nordell was so excited for us—yet he was apprehensive, too. We went over a thousand questions and then walked to the next room for an ultrasound. I couldn't believe I was going to see my baby—and so soon! I hadn't had an ultrasound with Alyssa because the doctors had not felt it necessary, and back then they just weren't routine.

During the ultrasound we narrowed down a due date—an actual due date. This made it so real for me. Somewhere around March 23, 2007, my second child would be born—a second miracle! To actually see my child on the ultrasound was amazing. That tiny life inside of me, to whom I was already feeling such a connection, was going to be the fulfillment of every dream I'd ever had. It is truly a precious gift from God that we, as women, can feel such a bond to the life growing within us. I felt as if I had known this baby my whole life and I couldn't imagine ever being without that little spirit.

We went over all the crazy medications and things that had happened to me over the last couple of months and then the doctor was very up-front with us. Things didn't look really good. I had always had female problems, but with the medications I was taking, plus my age, we just had to take things a day at a time. I remember thinking, *my age?* I was only thirty-four-years old—but that's considered borderline for having children.

I was labeled high risk and told to go home and take it easy. An appointment was set up for the next week, and I was told I would also be seeing a perinatologist who specializes in high-risk pregnancies. *Whatever,* I thought. I was going to have a baby! The rest of my life would be different from this moment on. I'd been having anxiety at the thought of my daughter leaving home for college within the next two years, but now I'd be okay because my dear, sweet hubby and I were going to raise a child together. I kept thinking of all the things I would do right by this baby, as if I had somehow been given a second chance to be a better mom.

I have never been able to figure out why the Lord gave Alyssa to me. She was so amazingly perfect and such a fantastic daughter, especially compared to what a horrible child and teenager I had been to my parents. I thought people were supposed to grow up and raise a child just like themselves, to teach them a lesson. But Alyssa was a princess to me. She was a beautiful, moral, virtuous young woman who knew exactly what she was going to do with her life. I can't take credit for her turning out so well—I think maybe the Lord knew I couldn't handle someone like myself, so He sent my sweet Alyssa Lee.

Perhaps the worst news of that doctor visit was that we really shouldn't get our hopes up too high. More than likely, this child would abort itself because I just wasn't good at having babies, and

I had done all kinds of things wrong during those first few weeks. I was a regular at Lagoon, an amusement park resort with wild rides. I also wiped out several times on Bear Lake while riding tubes behind boats. Put this all together with the stupid medications I had been on and I was one messed-up host for a baby.

Yet, why would God have sent us this amazing miracle? From the very first moment I realized I was going to have another child, I truly believed I would spend the rest of my life with my baby. The doctor and my husband kept telling me not to be surprised if I miscarried, but I never doubted. I agreed with everything they told me, but deep down I just couldn't believe the Lord would allow me to conceive and then take my child away from me. I wanted this baby more than life itself, and I would do whatever it took to get my child here.

I started seeing Dr. Nordell weekly. Every visit he seemed surprised I was fine. In spite of the fact that I was throwing up several times a day, everything looked perfectly normal. My baby was even growing at exactly the rate expected, but Chas still wanted me to keep quiet about it. He somehow convinced the doctor (at least that's what I firmly believe) that we couldn't tell anyone until I was out of danger. Dr. Nordell told me if I made it to the thirteenth week, I could tell everyone I wanted to. As if I wasn't going to make it? It always irked me how surprised he was at my progress. At that point, the only thing abnormal was the fact that I wasn't gaining any weight. But who could, when they were constantly throwing up?

Finally the thirteenth week arrived—the magic number—and the doctor told us we were past the point where we should worry about miscarriage.

He said, "Now keep in mind, you aren't out of danger and we need to keep a very close eye on things. But overall, everything looks great."

"You mean I can finally tell people?" I asked him.

"Yes, you can tell anybody and everybody if you want to."

I could finally tell people! Alyssa would be the first to know. I had her convinced I was throwing up all the time because of the medications I had to take. But we were worried about how she would take it.

A year before, I had come home from a doctor visit with a handful of samples. Dr. Nordell wanted me to start taking vitamins *and* birth control pills in order to regulate my PCOS. I threw the samples on the kitchen counter and started cleaning the house. A while later Alyssa was helping me. She seemed quiet. I asked her what was wrong, but she said nothing. That wasn't like her, so I prodded until she suddenly broke down crying.

"Are you pregnant?" she asked through her tears.

"Whoa! Would it be so bad if I were? That would be a miracle, sweetie!" I said. To say the least, I was shocked at her response.

She told me she had found the pills on the cupboard and she was confused, because they were prenatal vitamins and birth control pills. I explained what my doctor had said, and why he wanted me to take them.

She told me that even with my marriage to Chas, who brought in four step-children, she still felt like an only child and that was the way she liked it. You could say she was being selfish, but for sixteen years she had been the only one to receive my attention.

When we decided to tell her, we were sitting on the downstairs couch watching TV together. I figured the best way was to just lay it out there.

"I'm pregnant," I said.

"Are you kidding?" she asked. "Is this some kind of joke?"

"No, Lys. Remember how sick I've been lately? It's because I'm pregnant," I told her.

She sat there for a few moments, closed her eyes, took in a deep breath, and went to her room. Which, of course, made me upset so I started crying. I was doing a lot of that lately—those hormones are crazy to deal with. That, in turn, upset Chas because he wanted me to take it easy. He never liked seeing me troubled.

I tried to go talk to Alyssa, but she told me she needed some time to deal with things. So for the first time in a long time, I didn't tuck her in and kiss her goodnight. It was tough for me, because I so desperately wanted this child, but I hated seeing Alyssa so traumatized. I also couldn't understand why she wasn't happy. I knew life would change drastically, but that wouldn't change the way I treated or took care of my daughter. I finally came to the conclusion that she would never truly understand until she had children of her own, and there was still plenty of time before that happened.

The next morning Alyssa was still melancholy. She went

about her same routine, but just not with the same spunk she usually had. I realized there was nothing I could say or do, so I just had to wait for her to come to me. I went to school and went about my day. It was hard, but my students always have a way of bumping me out of sad moods, so I soon was teaching and enjoying the day.

Things were about the same at home that evening. Alyssa kept to herself and worked on her homework, while Chas and I cooked, cleaned, and watched some TV. While we were sitting on the couch, she walked in with a funny look on her face.

"I just wanted you guys to know I've fasted, prayed, and done a lot of thinking since you told me you were pregnant and I decided I'm okay with it."

This made Chas a little upset—I could tell from the tension in the air. I was thrilled she was coming around to the idea, but I was worried about Chas's reaction to how she had said it. Funny thing, teenagers—they just don't quite know how to express themselves properly. And Chas had little patience, not to mention any experience, with the teenage psyche.

"What do you mean, 'you're okay' with it?" he snapped. "Are you saying it's 'okay' if we go ahead and have this baby? Like we need your permission or something?"

"No, that's not what I meant," she replied. "I just mean that even though I've been a brat about this, I'm really okay with it. I'm just worried how we're going to afford having another kid. And where are we going to put it?"

"It? Are you kidding me?" I chimed in. I understood this was all a shock to her, but good grief—even for a teenager, she was going too far. "Aren't those problems for *us* to worry about? And this is a *child*—your *sibling*—not an 'it!'"

"No, mom! I didn't mean it like that. I'm sorry, I'm just so worried."

She was crying now, and clearly this wasn't going the way she had planned. I told her to come and sit down beside me and the rest of the evening was spent with apologies and explanations. All in all, we tried to reassure Alyssa this wasn't something to worry about. We always found a way to deal with life and live comfortably, so we would find a way again. And besides—this was a person, a new addition to our home. So what if life was a little tough at times? We had always been able to take care of our family, both mentally and physically.

Yes, we were all scared, but we knew the Lord had not sent us this precious spirit to be a burden. He was sending us our little baby to raise and have a good life.

*The road leading to a goal does not separate you from the destination; it is essentially a part of it.*

- Charles de Lint -

CHAPTER FIVE

# Sharing the News

The next few days were a whirlwind. I wanted to tell my mother, but she has a special way of not keeping things to herself. I wanted to be the one to tell my brothers, so I decided I would tell them first, and then let my mother know.

It was then I realized how much I truly missed my father. I was a daddy's girl through and through. But unfortunately, he wasn't around to share the news. My dad died at the young age of fifty-three in November of 2004.

To this day, it's hard for me to accept his death. It seems like I see my father everywhere and I dream about him quite often. I just keep thinking I'll see him coming down the road in his truck, or walking down the trodden path around his favorite fishing spot, or snuggled in with a blanket on his recliner to watch one of his favorite western shows. And now that I was going to give him another grandchild, a *miracle* grandchild, I couldn't even share my news with him. My child would never know its grandpa. But deep down, I believed my dad was in a better place and perhaps he would get to meet my child before coming to this earth. Maybe they were able to spend time together. If I didn't believe that, I think I would have lost my mind.

With thoughts of my dad on my mind, I decided to tell my brother Matt first. He had a son that would be turning one soon and I knew he would be so happy for me. I called him and said I needed to talk to him about something, but he was in a hurry—nothing new—so if I wanted to talk, I would have to meet him at the Subway restaurant and talk while he ate.

I met him inside and engaged in small talk while he ordered his meal. Then we sat down and I just blurted it out. "Well, I wanted to meet with you to tell you I'm pregnant."

His reaction was priceless. As he was raising his hand with the sandwich in it and his mouth was opening, he dropped the sandwich and his mouth stayed open.

He sat there for what seemed like a full minute and then he shook his head and asked, "Are you serious?"

I told him I was and his next reaction was a huge grin. I just love it when Matt smiles. He has a way of lighting up a whole room with just a smirk on his face and when he smiles, you know it's for real.

We talked for a while about how this was such a miracle and he made me feel really good when he told me he was happy his son would have a cousin around his age. It was so great to be around someone who could share in my joy! Up to this point, only my husband, the doctor, and I had known. I felt exhilarated to be able to share my news and feel of others' happiness. I asked Matt not to say anything for a couple of days until I could meet with Mom and let her know. I told him I would be telling my other brothers soon and he could for sure tell his wife. I knew she would be so happy for me as well.

We said our goodbyes and I called my oldest brother, Tony. He was also in a big hurry (once again, no surprise), so I told him I would run to his house and I only needed two minutes of his time.

As I was driving to his home, I passed him driving the other way. I guess he wasn't kidding when he said to hurry. I waved him down and he pulled over. I ran up to his truck and as he rolled the window down, I said, "Sorry to bug you, but I wanted to let you know I'm pregnant!"

His first reaction was, "Are you kidding me?"

He suddenly had time to stop and chat. Funny how life-changing events seem to put things in perspective and make you stop and feel the sunshine from time to time. I hopped in the cab of his truck and we talked for a while. It was so nice to let my family know. I hadn't been this happy in ages.

I gave Tony the same request to not say anything to Mom, and as I was leaving his truck, his wife and son came driving by. They pulled over and I got to share my news with them, too. She was so excited for me—and so was my eight-year-old nephew. The only thing I wasn't prepared for was her getting upset with me (sarcastically, of course) for not telling her sooner. My brothers hadn't even thought of that fact, yet it was one of the first things on her mind. I explained to her why—and she was still upset. She is not only my sister-in-law, but also one of my best friends. I have known her for over twenty years, and she was truly like the sister I never had growing up. I am very blessed to have her in my life.

We talked for a while about what to expect and she was genuinely happy for me. Then again, who wouldn't be? This amazing miracle was happening to my family. If only we had known what was soon to happen, then maybe, we could have prepared ourselves better.

*In all things of nature*
*there is something of the marvelous.*

- Aristotle -

CHAPTER SIX

# GRANDMA'S JOY AND TURMOIL

On my way home from talking to my brothers, I called my husband to ask his advice. I hadn't yet told my younger brother, Jed. He was a full-time soldier in the Army currently serving in Afghanistan. His wife was living on an Army post in Louisiana. I wouldn't be able to talk to Jed, so I would need to call his wife and she could relay the message to him. It broke my heart that I wouldn't be able to tell him in person. But it also broke my heart to tell them both my wonderful news when they had been trying for a child of their own for so long.

I asked Chas if he thought I should wait to tell them because I didn't want to make them feel bad, or make it look as though I was rubbing it in. I don't know what made me think these things—must have been the hormones—because they are both amazing people who would only want the best for me. Yet at the time, I hesitated. I was worried I would offend them.

To my surprise, Chas didn't give me the advice I was looking for. He was upset I had told my brothers without him.

"What made you think I wouldn't want to be there when they found out?" he asked.

"Oh, honey, I'm sorry. I truly had no idea you would want to be there. I just wanted to tell them so badly that I did. I really didn't know," I said.

"Whatever. I'll talk to you when I get home from work."

Then that was it. We hung up. I pulled over and cried for a few minutes. Everything was making me cry lately. But Chas was right. I had no business telling anybody without checking to see if he wanted to do it with me. It was rude of me, and by doing so, I was taking away one of the few things a father gets to be a part of in expecting a child. I couldn't figure out how I was going to make this up to him, so I pulled myself together and drove home. Telling Jed and his wife would have to wait.

Later that evening, after everybody was home, we decided it was time to tell my mother. I called her and asked if she was coming to town at all and, if so, could she stop by my house for something. It turned out she was going to visit my brother, Matt, who lived a mile from me, so she said she'd stop by before she went to his house.

Before she came over, I had to heal the rift that had formed between Chas and I. I can't stand it when he's upset with me, and I wanted to make things right.

"Chas, I know I messed up by telling my brothers without you. I really don't know why I didn't talk to you first," I said to him.

"I don't know why you thought I wouldn't want to be there

to begin with. This is a big deal and I want to share in everything. I don't get to have the same connection you do with our child, so every chance I get to share in something, it makes me feel more like a father," he said.

"I realize that now, but it just didn't occur to me at the time. I really have no excuse. Truth be told, I would love for you to have seen their reactions, and I'm sorry I took that away from you."

"Thanks for apologizing and letting me know you weren't trying to be mean. I understand your thoughts are all over the place right now—mine are and I'm not the one who is pregnant. Just try and remember me next time you want to share anything that has to do with our baby, okay?"

I apologized again and assured him I would talk to him more about things. I really felt horrible I hadn't included him.

Everyone in my family has a very sarcastic side, so we thought we would tease my mother a bit before letting her know. When she got there we were all sitting serenely on the couches and tried to act very solemn.

"Mom, we asked you to come over because we have some serious news to tell you," I said.

She looked concerned, but bewildered at the same time.

"They found a growth," I said.

"What? What are you talking about? On you?"

"Yes. They took a picture so you can see exactly where," I told her.

Then I gave her a picture of the ultrasound. She immediately understood the joke as I handed her the picture. She didn't even look at it, but instead, pushed it aside and gave me a big hug.

"How is this possible?" she asked. "You can't have any more children."

I explained to her everything that was going on. It was so nice to be able to tell her. But then she found out I had told my brothers before her. I told her as nicely as possible that *I* wanted to be the one to tell everyone. So we kept it from her until I had told those I wanted to—except Jed. I did give her permission to tell aunts, uncles, cousins, etc. I figured that would appease her, and quite frankly, I wanted *everyone* to know.

My sister, Katie, was with my mother when I told her and she was her usual jubilant self. Katie has a way of making everything around her seem like a party and it was nice to be able to feel her excitement.

I asked my mother's advice about telling Jed and his wife and she assured me they would be happy for me. Sure, they were having a hard time getting pregnant, but they would be extremely happy for us. So later that night, I called his wife and told her the news.

She was very excited for us. Shocked, but excited. She told me she would let Jed know the next time he called. I also sent him an email that night letting him know. I hated that I couldn't talk to him, but I had no choice. As expected, he was ecstatic about it. It's amazing how the birth of a child can make all those around so happy. Things couldn't be going better. That was, until our next doctor appointment.

I was losing weight, and quickly. This was to be expected with how much I was vomiting. I was to the point of throwing up several times a day and once or twice at night. We tried every trick imaginable and even a few medications. After much trial and error, we found that if I took an anti-nausea medication with milk and soda crackers, and ate something every hour, I could keep my vomiting to a minimum. I still threw up a couple of times a day, but I didn't care—anything to get my child here safely. Your perspective on life sure changes when you are carrying a child inside of you.

The next couple of months were as crazy as the first. My blood pressure was up and I was retaining water but losing weight. The vomiting was under control but was still very much there. However, someone told me that if you throw up a lot in pregnancy that meant it was a boy. I knew this was not valid medical advice, but I still held out hope it was true. Chas had five girls. I had one girl. It was time for some more testosterone in our household—even the dog was a girl.

Sure enough, in October, we found out we were having a boy. A baby boy! Words could not express my true joy in this. I would have been happy with a girl, but knowing this would definitely be my last child, I really wanted a little boy. Life couldn't have been better.

I went through the usual pregnancy misfortunes: exhaustion, emotional, and especially the vomiting. Throughout it all, though, I didn't care. I could feel this precious spirit growing inside of me, and I didn't care what physical ailments would befall me. I just couldn't wait for my baby boy to be here.

Also exciting was the small bump starting to show. Sixteen years earlier, when I was pregnant with Alyssa, I never showed enough to buy maternity clothes. Now my pants weren't fitting—it was so exciting. Other women were calling me crazy when all I could think about was showing everybody I was pregnant.

My mother took me shopping at a maternity store and bought me several outfits. They were so adorable! They fit comfortably and would be large enough to last me through all nine months.

Toward the end of October, I started feeling a sharp pain above the right side of my abdomen. It was random, so my doctor told me to keep watch for it and try to focus on where and when it occurred. I figured it was just another pregnancy ailment and went on with regular life.

We continued getting weekly ultrasounds and closely monitored my son's growth. He was progressing exactly as he should have been. My doctor kept being surprised that everything was okay, because of my history with my first child. But I knew in my heart that my son was special and nothing would happen to him. The Lord would not have sent me such a marvel and then take it away.

The weeks turned into November and I was getting more uncomfortable by the day. I voiced my concerns to my doctor, but all the tests and monitoring showed things as normal, including my son's growth. However, just in case, he scheduled an appointment with a perinatologist again.

Again, there were no problems. My son was as healthy as could be. In fact, he was so active they had a hard time getting measurements.

The second week of November proved to be my worst yet. The sharp pains I had felt before were increasing in both frequency and severity. One night as I was suffering, I had a sudden realization that I had felt similar pains a few years before when I was hospitalized for a week with pancreatitis. I wanted to make sure my baby was okay, so Chas and I drove to the emergency room.

After a few hours, many tests, and much anguish, the ER doctor determined I had a gall bladder problem. They convinced me to take some pain meds that wouldn't affect my son, but that would help alleviate my suffering. They assured me it would only make him sleepy.

Throughout that evening, I was miserable. But something amazing happened, too. I felt my son kick! I had never felt my daughter move, and had always felt I had missed something so important. It's funny to realize that the first time I felt my son move, I was sleepy and delirious on pain meds.

From that night on, I felt him move hourly. Nothing can compare to what it feels like to have your child move within you. There is nothing sweeter, more calming, and reassuring than having such a tiny little presence make such a huge impact on your life.

I went to my regular doctor that Monday and he concluded the same thing as the ER doctor. I had a bad gall bladder. Sometimes they can remove them during a pregnancy, but in my case, I was too high risk to chance surgery, so it would have to wait until my son was born. In the meantime, I was put on a no-fat diet. "No-fat" is *really* hard to do. I had no idea how much fat was in everything until I had to take notice.

Okay, truth be told, no fat is next to impossible. There is at least a little bit in everything, and to make matters worse, the foods I was supposed to eat were very expensive. It's funny how an item with less of something in it actually costs more. But we were willing to do anything, so we cut spending on other things and stocked up.

At this point, Chas was beginning to get excited for our son. He didn't say much before, only showing concern about me and my health, but now that I was showing it became more real for him. It was wonderful to see his excitement.

The doctors told me that any time I ate fat my gall bladder would react and cause me pain. They also informed me it was worse for the baby for me to be in pain than it was to be on pain killers. They prescribed Lortab to take when the pain got to be too much.

Over the next two weeks, I made four trips to the emergency room. Whether I ate fat or not, the pain was still there—and getting worse. I was still throwing up several times a day and I was overall miserable. Interestingly enough, I still felt overjoyed to be pregnant. Feeling my son move within me was pure bliss—I loved being pregnant. I started asking myself why women complain about pregnancy, when even though I was having multiple problems, I still loved it.

I was getting to be a regular at the hospital, to the point they knew me by sight. This was embarrassing, but sometimes the pain got so bad I just couldn't take it anymore. Each time I went, they gave me an IV and started pain meds. The baby was always doing fine, but at this point I was getting extremely frustrated.

I did a lot of research on the Internet about gall bladder problems in pregnancy. Nothing seemed to jive. I was having all of the symptoms that were listed, but I was eating between one to four grams of fat per day—and I read that I shouldn't be having the pain I was having with the lack of fat I was consuming. Something just wasn't quite right, yet every time I voiced my concerns to the doctor, he told me everything looked good.

We stopped getting weekly ultrasounds and just scheduled them monthly. This made me nervous. Not only did I want to make sure my baby boy was okay, I also loved seeing him move around so much on the TV screen. He was so active! Of course I was already imagining him on all sorts of sports teams: football, basketball, soccer, baseball, wrestling, etc. I just *knew* he would be a great athlete with all the moving around he did. Plus, my hubby is built athletically, so whenever I pictured my son, I pictured a younger version of my husband—tall, dark-haired, and handsome.

I still tried to find a pattern in all of the madness, but nothing seemed to make any sense. So I went on eating as little fat as I could while still giving my body and baby nutrition. Funny thing was, I lost weight when I was pregnant and gained it when I wasn't. I was finally starting to get that pregnancy glow everybody talks about, and I was fitting slimmer in all of my clothes. Except around the waist, of course. If only I could go back to that time, back when my 'glow' was bright and not dim.

*But thou, oh Lord,*
*art a shield for me;*
*my glory, and the lifter up*
*of mine head.*

- Psalms 3: 3 -

## CHAPTER SEVEN

# TENSION

The next week I had another appointment with the specialist, but this time I went to a bigger hospital in a larger city. They had new equipment and higher levels of technology that could assist the doctors better in making sure my baby was doing well.

My hubby and I decided to take the entire family to this appointment. The kids were excited to see the baby for the first time. We made the hour-long drive with excitement and anticipation. I was feeling great, besides still throwing up, and I couldn't wait to see my son again!

The appointment lasted about an hour. I was a little intimidated having my naked belly showing for everybody, but seeing my son on the monitor and seeing him move around was worth it. They took several pictures that were so adorable. You could see his silhouette, sucking his thumb, and at one point, even his tiny little foot pressing against my belly. Was this true bliss? I couldn't believe something so small could make a room full of people breathless.

Everything looked great, according to the doctor. He didn't seem concerned about my gall bladder pain, or my throwing up, or anything else. My son was growing at the exact rate he should have been. However, I still had this nagging feeling things just weren't quite right. I couldn't figure why, so I chalked it up to being nervous. After all, it had been seventeen years since I had been pregnant. I was technically a newbie at this.

We left the hospital and took the kids out to eat. I got a sandwich that didn't have much fat in it, and felt great. We loaded up the van and started home. Not five minutes into the drive, that same miserable pain that had become my enemy returned.

I reclined the seat and tried my best to alleviate it. Nothing worked. So I took another pain med and tried to sleep. This worked for a time, and after we got home that evening, I went to bed and tried to block out the pain. Knowing I was enduring this for my son made it easier to bear.

Over the next few weeks I made a couple more trips to the ER and tried my best to manage the pain. At this point, things started to weigh down on my relationship with my husband. I wondered if he didn't believe me about the pain because he started getting short with me. He was also upset that I was still losing weight. He thought I wasn't eating enough, and I felt like I was. I felt like nobody was helping me keep the house clean and he felt like if I cared more for my son, I wouldn't be cleaning as much. The tension was so thick you could feel the weight of it. As if it was an unseen presence in the air. I realized I was extra sensitive and Chas was stressed about me and our son.

At one point in the early hours of one December morning, I hadn't slept the entire night because of the pain, so I woke Chas up and told him I needed to go to the hospital again.

He asked me, "Again? Are you sure? Do you need me to drive you?"

I couldn't believe the question, which immediately put me on the defense, so I of course said, "No. I can drive just fine. Go back to sleep and I'll see you when I get back."

"Okay, let me know if you need anything," he said. "Also, Alyssa could go with you if you want."

I left in a hurry, appalled that he wasn't coming with me. This solidified my theory that he didn't believe me. However, I hadn't made it three blocks down the street before he called my cell phone.

"Hon, have you left?"

"Of course, I have. I can't take it anymore! They have to be able to do something. This just isn't normal!" I was screaming and crying at the same time.

"Come back home and I'll drive you. You left when I was still half asleep and I didn't think you were serious."

I turned around, thankful for his phone call, and we made yet another ER trip

After I was there for a few hours and my pain was under control, we went back home. I thought it was just crazy that another ER doctor said my gall bladder looked fine on the ultrasound, yet that was where my pain was located. I cried and cried in the hospital room that time, out of frustration, pain, fear, and feeling so helpless. I knew this wasn't normal for a pregnancy. Plus to top it all off, I wasn't keeping much of anything down, so how was my baby supposed to get nourishment?

At that point, I was just trying my best to make it to Christmas break. School is very stressful during December, and I needed to make it through that time to be able to get some rest and relaxation. So I continued on that crazy diet, having some good days and more often bad ones, and trying my best to take care of myself.

The break finally came, and I was able to get the rest I so desperately needed. Chas and I were still fighting and arguing daily, but I had my pain under control. I started having a hard time breathing with any level of activity, but otherwise I was doing okay.

I saw my doctor again the day after Christmas, and he determined it was time for me to be put on bed rest. I was devastated but I knew it had been coming. I'm not a TV kind of person, and the thought of staying cooped up in my bed all day was depressing. But I was determined to do anything and everything for my son.

I started preparing for being on bed rest for three months. Three months! That was such a long time to be bedridden. I was so grateful for my laptop at that time. I was able to arrange for a long-term sub at school and, thankfully, I had thought this might happen, so I prepared a lot for my classroom in advance. My sub would not have to worry about lesson plans for a while and the other teachers would gladly help. It was almost a relief that all I had to do was take care of me and my baby. Other than the fact our income would now be cut in half, things were looking good.

Christmas break was wonderful. It was so nice to be able to relax and take care of myself. I was getting to know my little baby more and more because I was able to focus intently on his every move. There is nothing in this world that can compare to the joys and rapture you feel when you are truly focusing on that precious life inside of you.

I continued my fat-free diet and tried my best to relax. And of course I was focusing on everything 'baby.' I wanted to go shopping and get our son's room together. It's said a woman gets a nesting feeling when she's pregnant and wants to clean and make everything perfect for her new little one. I felt the desire to make sure *everything* was perfect for my little boy. Yet my husband kept saying we had plenty of time.

He and I had disagreed from the beginning about the baby even having his own room. Chas thought we could wait until he was older, and for the time being he could just stay in our room. I was determined to raise my child right—which included proper sleeping habits. Chas leaves for work at four in the morning; not exactly conducive to a baby trying to sleep. Plus, all of our bedrooms were completely girly. I so desperately wanted my son to have a boyish and rugged room.

"Why can't we just have two of the girls share a room? It's not going to hurt them to share and that way our son can have his own room, right next to ours," I said.

"I just think you are moving too quickly. We have plenty of time to get things ready, and I worked hard to get our house built so each child could have their own room. Our son won't know the difference until he gets older," Chas said.

"Good grief! This is ridiculous. We don't have the space for him in our room, and I want him to have his own room—why can't you understand that?"

"Amy, we'll talk about this another time. Quit worrying about it right now. We have plenty of time to get things ready."

I kept pestering him about it, and after much complaining, Chas finally agreed the twins could share a room or one of them could turn the computer room into her bedroom. I nagged him quite often about getting it done, but to no avail. I clearly couldn't do it on my own, because I was supposed to be taking it easy, so I just had to wait. At least I got him to agree to the arrangement—one small victory.

In the meantime, I had dear friends bringing me adorable baby clothes and hand-me-downs. I took great pride in washing them, folding them, and placing them neatly in bins ready for unloading in my new baby's room. I sat for the longest time just smelling the clothes and feeling the textures of the blankets that would be next to my child's smooth skin. I envisioned him wearing them and me holding him while we snuggled and giggled together.

I was convinced at this point I needed to stay home with my precious one until he was old enough to go to school. I loved teaching, but I had to put my family first, and this little boy needed his mama. Truth be told, I needed him more than he needed me, but I wouldn't truly realize this truth until much too late.

The other thing Chas and I argued about during this time was something I was doing and not realizing. Chas and I were getting ready for a family party on Christmas Day. My daughter was visiting her father's family, and my step-children were with their mother. We were going to pick the girls up and attend a party that was an hour and a half away.

I don't even remember why we were arguing, but once we started, it didn't stop. We continued bickering the entire morning, to the point that he left the house and told me he was going to the party without me. This only made me more upset because I had cleaned the house, showered and primped, prepared food to take, and was looking forward to doing something different. So much for bed rest.

After much text messaging and phone calling, he finally came home with just enough time to spare to get going for the party. We decided to go and talk about it on the way. It turned out I had been so focused on our baby, I had completely neglected being a mother to my step-children and a wife to my husband. He couldn't understand why I had even wanted to go to the party when I didn't care about them or anything that didn't have something to do with the baby.

It was true, however, that my every moment was spent thinking of my son. Countless numbers of times I played over and over in my mind the future we would have together. It's amazing, but by the time I was six months pregnant, I felt like I had lived an entire life with my unborn child, simply because of the massive amount of daydreaming I had done.

I realized from this point on, I had to focus on my family *and* taking care of myself. I was sure the arguing couldn't be doing anything good for my blood pressure. At each doctor's appointment my blood pressure was unusually high. My doctor assumed it had to do with the pain I was suffering from the gall bladder problems, so it was nothing to worry about. But still, it wasn't good for me or the baby. Things would have to change, and soon.

We got things set up more permanently in our bedroom, making it easier to help me survive the next three months on complete bed rest. I was only allowed to get up to use the bathroom and shower. I only lasted a few days before I thought I was going to lose my mind. I knew this was the best thing to do, but I was so stir-crazy, I just couldn't think straight anymore.

By that Friday, the pain in my side had become so intense, I knew I had to go back to the hospital. Our doctor had told me that I was in danger of preeclampsia and to start watching for the signs. When he described the symptoms to me, I looked at him funny because it was exactly what I had been going through. He told me it would be similar to the gall bladder pain, but different, so I would know if something was wrong. Well, nothing was different with the pain, but I *knew* my baby was somehow in danger.

Once again, we got ready to go to the ER. This was on a Friday evening and, luckily, my doctor was on call that weekend, so we phoned him. He made the decision to admit me to the Women's Center and keep me there for a few days of observation.

I thought to myself, *finally! We're going to find out what's wrong and make things right!*

My step-children were staying with us for the remainder of the Christmas break, so we brought them with us so they could feel involved. We figured it would be another routine visit to the hospital with possibly more tests being run this time.

*I will not be made useless, I won't be idled with despair,*
*I will gather myself around my faith, for light does the*
*darkness most fear. My hands are small,*
*I know, but they're not yours they are my own.*

- Lyrics from "Hands" by Jewel -

## CHAPTER EIGHT

# WHIRLWIND

I purposefully packed a small bag of toiletries and reading material with the sole purpose of jinxing Murphy's Law and making our stay a short one. We got to the hospital, and unlike so many other visits, this time they put me in a wheel chair and admitted me to a beautiful room. The nurses who worked on that floor were amazing. They were so kind, gentle, and loving, treating me as if I was their only patient.

Their first order of business was to set up a fetal monitor. This contraption straps around your belly and stays put so your baby's heartbeat can always be watched and heard. It was wonderful to hear that little thump! However, my son did not like that funny round thing poking on him. He started kicking it as soon as they put it on. It was a constant kick, like he thought if he hit it enough times, they would remove it. Finally, my husband was able to feel our son's kicks! And not only feel them, but see them and hear it on the monitor. He thought it was cute, but I started to feel bad, as if it was somehow uncomfortable for the baby. That 'mama bear' instinct was kicking in fiercely—and I was feeling helpless. I knew it was something ridiculous for me to be fretting about, yet I couldn't quit worrying until he stopped. He kicked that monitor for at least five minutes until he became resolved to the fact that it was staying put and he would have to share space with it.

After an hour or so, our doctor showed up and started looking at all of the testing they had done. Everything looked good. At that point, he decided I could go home and just keep a close eye on everything. My pain had once again gone away and my blood pressure was back to normal. I was excited to go home, but let down that we still didn't know why these things were happening.

At the last minute, the doctor decided to order a quick ultrasound to take a look at the baby and see what was going on inside. We waited for the technician to come and Chas took the girls down to the cafeteria for some food.

The doctor did the usual measurements, looked around and made sure everything was okay, and I was relieved to see my little boy again. He looked perfect and exuberant, moving around like a mini trapeze artist. Then the technician said something that is still engraved firmly in my mind.

"He looks great! You're about twenty-four weeks along, right?" he asked.

I said, "What? You mean twenty-eight weeks? I'm twenty-eight weeks along." Then I started looking at the measurements on the screen. They were all reading a twenty-four week-old baby.

"Everything measures as though he is twenty-four weeks along, but I'll double check just to make sure," he said.

So I waited through another round of measurements. All the while he kept saying, "Yep, just what I thought, twenty-four weeks."

"What does that mean? That he's just little? He was fine at my last ultrasound, measuring exactly how he should have been."

"You'll have to wait and talk to your doctor. I'm just the technician, and I don't diagnose anything. I'm sure he'll be up to talk to you soon," he said.

So again, I waited. By the time the doctor came into my room, Chas was back with the girls and we were waiting to hear what was going to happen. The last thing the nurses told us was that I would be going home for at least the weekend, so we made plans for exactly that. Then Dr. Nordell told us things weren't looking good.

Basically, our son had stopped growing. He was still surviving in the womb, but his growth had slowed so much, the doctor had to consider the real possibility that I had severe preeclampsia and there was actually no gall bladder problem. He ordered a catheter be placed so they could collect my urine and test it. After twenty-four hours they could run some tests on it to see whether or not I had preeclampsia and how severe it was.

Chas took my hand in his and said, "What can I do for you, sweetie?"

"Call my mom," I told him. Even though I am a grown woman, whenever I am sick or in trouble, I always turn to my mother for comfort. So Chas called my mom and asked her to come to the hospital. Plus, it would really help to have someone to entertain the kids while we were dealing with all of this.

Next thing I knew, my mom, sister, and daughter were all in my room herding everybody out. My mother had nursing experience from long ago, and she knew that with preeclampsia you needed a quiet, dark, controlled room where there was no stress.

After about an hour, the doctor and everybody came back in my room. He told us he had been on the phone for almost that entire hour talking to the doctors at LDS Hospital and going over my information and history. Then he said something I had been completely unprepared for.

"You need to be life-flighted to their hospital in Salt Lake City. If you are indeed at a stage of severe preeclampsia, your son will have to be delivered early," he said.

I couldn't believe he was so calm. He continued telling us how twenty-eight weeks is a good point for delivery if the mom and baby are in danger. I argued with him and everybody around me that it was way too early—I wanted him to stay in me longer. I didn't care about the pain. I apologized profusely about complaining and promised everyone I wouldn't say anything else from that point on.

Dr. Nordell explained it wasn't my decision to make, because the next symptom with preeclampsia would be severe seizures that could kill both my baby and me.

So at that point I convinced myself I could make it though this and they would find out it wasn't preeclampsia after all or that it wasn't severe enough to deliver this early. Sure, the tears were flowing freely from everybody in the room, but I resolved that this was only a 'hiccup' in an ongoing battle to get my son here. I would, once again, do whatever it took to get my little boy delivered safely.

*What you spend years building may be destroyed overnight. Build anyway.*

- Mother Teresa -

## CHAPTER NINE

# AN AMAZING FLIGHT

They started prepping me for the flight to Salt Lake City. The staff was very helpful and friendly, yet I couldn't help but see the scared look on their faces each time someone would come in my room to check on me or make some sort of arrangement. I wanted to scream at them, *What's the matter with you! Nothing's wrong! We're just going on a short trip and in a few months I'll be back here delivering my perfect baby boy!*

A nurse came in to get my IV going. I warned her my veins didn't usually cooperate, but she assured me she was a pro and there wouldn't be a problem. After three tries on both arms, another nurse came in to help, but to no avail. They determined I needed a good large vein in case I had to go in for emergency surgery, so they called in the anesthesiologist to get it going. Chas had gone down to the cafeteria again with the younger kids and my daughter and sister, so it was just my mother and me in the room with the nurse and doctor.

After looking all over my arms, he warned me I needed to

concentrate very hard on not moving, because it was going to hurt. The nurse interrupted him and asked if she could numb the skin first, but he told her that usually hurt worse than the IV itself. She looked doubtful, but knew her place, too. I got a little concerned, but I had been poked so many times with needles over the last six months, I figured I could handle anything.

Then he tried to get a vein. I let out such a high, blood-curdling scream, three nurses came running in my room from down the hall. He dug for a vein, not having much luck. I had never felt such immense pain from an IV insertion and even my mother and the nurses had to look away from what he was doing.

He told me to stop moving or I would make it worse. "It's not that bad. You need to stop crying," he said.

"I'm trying the best I can, but this is insane! I have never had this kind of pain from a simple IV."

"Just hold still so I can concentrate."

I was silently praying Chas would come in at that moment and knock him off his chair. I had never met a doctor so rude. I realized later that he was just frustrated, as was everyone in the room, but he continued to dig while I screamed and begged him to stop. He finally did just to give me a break and find a different vein.

The fiasco continued on my other arm, until at last he got a vein. I was exhausted from the pain, and the poor nurses had to spend the next ten minutes cleaning up all the blood and mess he had made getting it in. The nurse who suggested the numbing medicine came to my bed side and apologized.

"I'm so sorry you had to go through that. I should have

insisted he let me numb your arm first." She was recovering from crying herself.

"It's not your fault; please don't apologize. I'm sorry I couldn't deal better with the pain," I replied. I was truly embarrassed that I had been crying and screaming. Then my husband came back. He was there just in time to see them cleaning up, and my mom brought him up-to-date on what had happened.

"Why didn't you send for me?" he asked me as he took my hand in his and wiped my tears from my cheeks.

"I thought you would be back at any moment and I wasn't thinking straight because of the pain," I told him.

"I'm so sorry I wasn't here to stop him. You know I wouldn't have let him do that."

I assured Chas I wasn't upset with him. The whole situation was just ugly. What more could you say? But I was still determined everything was going to be just fine. It never crossed my mind that my baby wouldn't be okay.

A few minutes later everything sped up like we had pushed fast forward on the DVD player. Two flight nurses came into my room and started hooking me up to all kinds of machines and talking to me about my situation. They were absolutely amazing at what they did. It takes a special person to be a flight nurse and these two must have been the cream of the crop. They made me feel like I was being checked into the Presidential Suite at a fancy hotel. Their kindness was almost overwhelming.

As they started wheeling me out of the room I saw my doctor standing in the doorway next to my mother. He looked dejected and miserable and I wondered why. It just seemed out of place and unnecessary. Such a faraway look for such a hurried, rushed time. Later, my mother would tell me the words he said to himself as he stood there.

Dr. Nordell said, "I can't believe I missed this. I can't believe I didn't know what was going on the whole time. I should have known."

My mother tried to reassure him, telling him, "Oh, I'm sure everything will be just fine. Don't you worry—Amy is a strong-willed person with complete faith."

I *am* a strong-willed person and I was positive everything would be great. I just had to get my baby in my arms where he would be safe and sound, and then life would begin again.

My husband walked with us through the hospital to get to the helicopter pad. I had walked the halls of this exact hospital so many times, but this time, I was the one getting sympathetic and frantic stares. I realized my situation must have looked grim—two flight nurses, Air Med packs on top of my gurney, a family of eight following closely behind, with a doctor and three nurses in tow. My situation looked dismal. Yet, all I thought was, *this will be a great memory to tell my son—both of my children flew on a helicopter before they were born.*

Before Alyssa's birth, we flew on a military helicopter. Cramped with a nurse, a doctor, and two pilots, I was in labor with a sticky, sweaty helmet crammed on my head. It was a miserable thirty minute flight. Luckily, we arrived without

Alyssa coming early, and three days later I gave birth to a beautiful, healthy little girl. I had no reason to believe this miracle would be any different. After all, the advances in technology since then were amazing.

They loaded me onto the helicopter and my husband captured it all with the built-in camera on his phone. I thought it odd at the time, and even teased him for it later, but now I love looking at those moments on film. I've learned the past couple of years to always have a camera ready. You never know when a memory needs to be captured on film. I may drive people crazy with my camera and camcorder, but you can never have too many pictures.

The flight nurses were amazing. There is simply no other way to put it. They situated me by a window so I could see out, talked to me constantly, told me everything that was going on, and acted like they had known me my whole life. I felt like my baby and I were the most important people on the planet. At one point, they told me to look out my window and I'll never forget the sight I beheld. It was sunset. I was flying just above the snow-capped mountains and it was breathtaking. It's true when they say, "God paints with *all* His colors." We couldn't say anything—to do so would have broken into the sweet, awe inspiring view around us. I couldn't wait to tell my son about the beautiful view I was lucky enough to see while on route to welcome him to the world. The mountains gave a perfect image of "purple mountain majesties." The air looked crisp and clear, and the colors in the clouds were beyond counting. Every shade of pink, orange, red, blue, purple, white, and yellow blended into an image of perfection.

We touched down at LDS Hospital in Salt Lake City around twenty-five minutes later. Unfortunately, it would take my husband and family a few more hours to get there. I was rushed into the hospital, and quickly put in a small, cramped room. The nurses explained I was only around the corner from the helicopter pad, and I wouldn't have to worry about other patients and people seeing me. Had I looked that bad? I assumed they were just trying to make me feel better, so I brushed it off as common courtesy.

I couldn't believe how small the room was. I almost gave in to a wave of claustrophobia, but talked myself out of it. I figured I wouldn't be in there long enough for it to be a problem. At the time I didn't realize I would be spending the next two days in there. Either way, I was determined to make the best out of this situation.

The nurses pumped me full of magnesium sulfate to lower my blood pressure and prevent the preeclampsia from getting any worse. They warned me it was a horrible medicine to be on and the last thing they do unless absolutely necessary. I truly did not care. They also gave me steroid shots every twelve hours to help my baby's lungs develop quicker.

Everything was being done to prepare me to give birth to a twenty-eight week-old baby. Since Alyssa was born at thirty-one weeks, I had no doubt my son would be just fine, but I still wanted him in me as long as possible. A highly-specialized pediatric doctor came in to talk to me about what to expect and

I kept telling her, "It's way too early for my son to be here. I'm planning on keeping him inside me as long as possible."

"But you have to prepare for what may happen if he does come early. And there is no way at this point that you will carry to full-term. We are just trying to let you know of every possible outcome," she said.

She politely listened to me give my reasons why I shouldn't give birth yet, nodding her head as I spoke, as if she were talking to a child. I assume that's what I must have seemed like, insisting things would go back to the way they were.

They hooked me up to the fetal heartbeat monitor and collected blood samples. I was starting to feel very alone when my mother showed up. I was surprised she had made it down before Chas did, but then again, I shouldn't have been. She was, after all, my mother, and this was not only her child in the hospital, but her grandchild.

It was nice to have her there to help the nurses take care of me. She was there for the birth of my first child, as well. She and my oldest brother made a day-long drive to California when I went into labor with Alyssa. They made the trip in ten hours instead of thirteen. Thank goodness for family!

I used my cell phone to call Chas and see why he wasn't there. He'd had to stop by our home and feed the girls, plus they all had to get some things ready for the drive. So it was a few hours before he was there, but things were going well and there was no need for him to hurry.

By this time, the mag sulfate was making me sick, tired,

and ornery. I'm a happy-go-lucky kind of person and I hated it when I got moody, but there was no avoiding it. The medicine was just too overpowering. The doctors and nurses informed me that after the twenty-four-hour urine test was complete, they would run a test to determine how severe the preeclampsia was. If it wasn't severe, I could be sent home on bed rest. Or, if it was slightly severe, I would stay in the hospital for a while until I delivered. I started praying and begging the Lord for the latter to happen. I knew it just wasn't time for my son to join us on earth. He needed a little longer in the oven before he was ready.

After a few hours, Chas finally arrived, but things were more stressful after that. We were all in a tiny little cramped room with four girls going stir-crazy. The nurses ended up shooing most everybody out of the room, but that also meant Chas had to leave to take care of the kids.

I rested for a while, during which Chas made arrangements with his brother to take care of the girls overnight. He and my mom slept in chairs in my room, tossing and turning while keeping watch over me. It was a very long night, to say the least.

The next day I felt better and hoped they would let me go home. However, it wasn't meant to happen that way. They got the test results and, sure enough, my preeclampsia was at a severe level. I was borderline of becoming eclamptic. A team of doctors determined I would need to go through an emergency Caesarean delivery to save both our lives.

*We'll do it all, everything, on our own.*
*We don't need anything, or anyone.*
*If I lay here, if I just lay here,*
*would you lie with me and just forget the world?*

- LYRICS TO "CHASING CARS"

AS SUNG BY SNOW PATROL -

CHAPTER TEN

# DECISIONS TO BE MADE

Everything went very fast from that moment on. Nurses and doctors rushed in and out of my room, running tests, prepping me, letting us know what was going on and what to expect, and then everything slowed down as if I was running in slow motion. I felt as though I was suddenly thrust into a dream world where you run and run but never get anywhere. I felt sluggish and drowsy. The room around me seemed to close in until it was barely big enough to contain me and my bed.

I felt as if I was screaming but nobody was hearing me. All sorts of people were running back and forth, poking me and prodding me, acting as though life were about to stop.

I finally could take no more and yelled, "What's going on?"

Those around me stopped and stared as if they suddenly noticed I was there. Then they got a look of concern and pity on their faces.

"Why does this have to happen? I feel fine and my son is doing great on the monitors. There is no need to do this!"

My mom was the first to come to my bedside. "Sweetie, you

aren't fine. If the baby stays in you any longer, there is a chance you will both die. I can't put it any more plainly than that."

"But I feel fine. None of this makes any sense to me. He is most definitely not ready to come. He needs to stay in me longer. I don't want him taken too early. I want to be pregnant. I want to go full term and deliver my son like all the other women. I want this experience. Can't you all understand that?" It seemed like I was rambling on and on.

At that point, one of my nurses took my hand in hers, and tried to explain to me what I still have a hard time understanding. The next possibility in preeclampsia is seizures. When and if that happened, it could kill the baby and me. Before that happened, they needed to deliver him so we both had a chance at surviving. She asked me if I wanted to talk to one of the doctors and I told her yes.

First, the doctor who was going to deliver my son came in and talked to us. She went over everything, step-by-step. Next, the doctor who would be taking care of him after he was born came in and explained what we could expect. I was twenty-eight weeks along, which was good. The main worry was that he was so little. On the ultrasound, they determined he weighed around one pound six ounces. So tiny!

I finally realized I had no other choice when the doctor explained that my body was no longer doing what my baby needed me to do for him. He was surviving, but not thriving. They estimated he had stopped growing around three weeks previously.

In other words, my body had failed him. It had gotten him this far, but no longer was it providing what he needed to grow. His only chance at this point was to have advanced medical care to grow and develop outside of the womb.

I took all of this in as well as I could and then turned my mind over to the realization that I was going to deliver my son that night. It was New Year's Eve and I was going to have a baby! What a wonderful way to ring in the New Year.

My next worry was the fact we still had not decided on a name. Chas and I had tossed around ideas for months. We had even gone to Border's and searched books for hours on end, hoping something would grab our attention. Every time Chas thought up a name, I had some objection. As a teacher, you begin to associate a particular behavior with a particular name. This makes it very difficult when picking out your own children's names. If behaviors don't play into it, then ridicule does. I found myself picking apart every name out there to determine if there was some way my child could be teased.

Then every time I thought of a good name, Chas didn't like it. We were here in the hospital, about to give birth to our son, and we didn't have a name for him.

I said to Chas, "Honey, I will not have my son come into this world without a name. We have to decide now."

To my surprise, he agreed. His sister was there, along with his mother. She produced several sheets of name ideas she had found in the hospital and I started circling the ones I liked. I showed the list to Chas and he wouldn't have anything to do with it.

"How can you just choose a name for our son off a random list?"

"We have to decide on something and I don't have any new ideas, do you?"

"We need to choose, but I don't want to pick something just because we feel rushed," he said.

So I kept looking at the list while he got on the phone to make other arrangements for our new little one coming soon.

He had to make sure the girls were taken care of and asked family members back home to start getting my son's room ready.

As I was looking at the choices I had circled, one in particular stood out—Connor. I tried to pick it apart, coming up with any reason he could be teased. Did it sound too feminine? Could anyone mispronounce it? Did it rhyme with something weird or abnormal?

Then I said it out loud. "Connor Charles Maddocks. It's perfect."

The one thing we had agreed upon was that he would have his daddy's name for his middle name. Chas had argued previously we didn't have to use his name, but I insisted and he finally relented.

When I said it out loud, everyone that was in the room agreed that it was a strong name. I kept saying it in my head, over and over. It was perfect. When Chas was done on the phone, I asked him to look at the list again. I showed him the name Connor, and repeated it out loud for him to hear.

"Don't you just love it?" I asked him.

For the first time, he agreed. I could see him running through his mind all of the possibilities that I already had and he finally said, "Yeah, I do like it."

I called Alyssa, who was still back home, and had her look up the name in the baby book we had bought. I wanted to know what it meant. She came back with the meaning and then I knew it was the right name. "Connor" means "lover of wolves." I love animals, and wolves are strong creatures. So it was decided. My son finally had a name. Chas filled out all of the paperwork for the birth certificate and it was official.

He kept asking me if I was sure, and kept restating we didn't need to give him "Charles" for a middle name, so I kept reassuring him it was right. After all, this would be my husband's first and only son. In my opinion, a son should have something in his name that has to do with his father. I knew Chas was still worried he wouldn't be a good enough dad, but I had faith he would be the best daddy Connor could have.

The next few hours went by with much anticipation, but I felt calm. My mother tried talking to me several times about how I needed to be prepared for what might happen, but I didn't understand what she was saying. Either I was in denial of the severity of the situation, or the medication I was on was making me oblivious of the predicament I was in.

All I could think about was the fact that my son would be in this world with me soon, and I could start a new life with my new baby.

My room was a whirlwind of motion, with people constantly coming in and out while poking and prodding me. It was as though everyone was in fast-motion, while I was observing the movement around me as if I was the only thing standing still in the room. Images and scents floated past my senses so quickly, and yet in my own personal bubble—life stood still.

I would sit on the bed and watch as though I was in the middle of a spinning carousel and I was the center holding it all together.

*There are two ways to live your life.*
*One is as though nothing is a miracle.*
*The other is as if everything is.*

- Albert Einstein -

CHAPTER ELEVEN

# BABY MEETS WORLD

It was getting close to the time when they were going to take me into the delivery room. The nurses came in and helped me lean back while they washed my hair. I didn't realize how crazy I looked until they gave me a mirror. Fashion just wasn't on my agenda the last few days, and it showed. The hair washing felt wonderful. They treated me as though I was in a salon and being pampered.

Next they wanted to change my bed sheets. They said when I came back I wouldn't feel up to moving around, so they needed to change them now. They lined up my husband, mother, and two nurses to help me move three feet over to a chair. I remember wondering why they thought I needed so much help, but I was soon to find out. The muscles in my legs were useless.

As the four helpers were trying to get me to the chair, I started to panic. Someone had failed to tell me the medicine I was on would make the muscles in my body feel as though they had atrophied. I started crying as soon as I got seated.

"What's going on? Why can't I walk? Am I going to be able to walk when Connor is born?"

One of the nurses said, "You'll be fine once you have this medicine out of your system. It's a nasty drug that messes with your body, but it isn't permanent."

"So am I going to need therapy to walk again?"

At that moment, everyone in the room started to laugh. They thought it was so funny I would think that. They were used to this stuff—I wasn't. This was new to me and all I knew was that my legs didn't work.

I started noticing the rest of my body. I had been feeling sick, but now came the realization that my body was far from my own. I had a look of panic and utter disbelief on my face, so the nurses and my mother tried to reassure me (without laughing) that I would be fine after a few days of being off the medicine.

"What do you mean, a few days? I need to be with my baby after he's born. I need to be up and around to be with him, because he will be in the NICU."

The nurses both explained to me it would be several days before the effects of the preeclampsia would be gone and I would be safe from those effects. Same for the mag sulfate. It would be a few days until that drug was completely out of my system. I would be able to be with Connor. I would just have to use a wheelchair for that week.

I calmed down and felt better after they had explained all of this to me. I was certain Connor would just be working on getting bigger and stronger during that time, so I needed to be with him every chance I had. The thought still didn't cross my mind that he would have any problems. I was just certain he would be fantastic.

Within the next hour, a few doctors came into my room to go over what to expect and what needed to be done. Each one talked to me about getting my tubes tied. Chas and I had talked about this before because we realized I wasn't very good at being pregnant. Connor was fulfilling all our dreams, so it would naturally make sense to have them tied. Yet something made me hesitate. Chas wasn't with me when the doctors came in, so I told them I would need to wait and talk to him.

One of the doctors told me she would get the paperwork ready so all I would need to do was sign. She went into great detail about how it may kill me and my child if I ever got pregnant again. They had never seen signs of preeclampsia so soon in a pregnancy and after going over my daughter's birth records, they had reason to suspect I may have had her early because of the same thing.

After hearing this from my doctors, several nurses, and my family, I figured it was the best thing to do. That type of decision is hard for a woman to make. I felt as though my womanhood was going to be taken away. As females, we are given the precious gift of bringing souls into this world and I don't think many women make the decision to take that gift away lightly. I kept telling myself it was for the best, but I still felt like I wouldn't be the same person.

Chas came in later and we talked about it. He agreed with everybody else; I needed to get my tubes tied. Then again, this would be his sixth child—so he felt he was done having kids. This would be my second—I still wanted more. But reason won this battle and I signed the papers allowing the doctors to do the procedure. My mother was probably the most happy; she worried constantly about me, and this would remove one worry from her troubled mind.

So now all we had to do was wait. The surgery was pushed back a couple of times for more emergency Caesarean deliveries. I didn't mind; I had waited years for this to happen. I could wait a few hours more.

The time finally came to go to the delivery room. Chas and my mother were both able to come with me and I will be forever grateful for having them there. It was hard for Chas to be comfortable letting my mom come, but I think he realized I needed all the support I could get. If I was delivering normally, it would have been just me and him; but this was different. So we went to the delivery room to say hello to our little Connor.

I have a newly discovered respect for women who go through C-sections. I had always believed that was the easy way out of deliveries. I was proud my first child had been born naturally and always wondered why a woman would have a

Caesarean if she had a choice. All you had to take care of was a little scar and then you were done—nothing like going through a vaginal delivery. How utterly wrong I was.

Delivering a baby through surgery was a terrible experience for me. I didn't have to work at all to get my child here—the main thing I did was focus on breathing. The entire time I felt like a turkey being gutted and stuffed for Thanksgiving dinner. I could feel everything they were doing, yet it wasn't painful. However, just knowing what they were doing made me have to concentrate on not throwing up. I wasn't able to savor the moment and take in the experience. I had to focus hard on what seemed like staying alive at the time.

Little Connor didn't want to come out yet. He was playing hide-and-seek with the doctors. They finally found him up as high as he could go and when they took him out, I heard the sweetest, most tender and precious sound I have ever heard—or will ever hear. He sounded like a little kitten meowing. The relief that came over me at that moment was like taking a one-hundred pound dumbbell off my chest. I didn't realize until that moment how much stress I had been under. My son was here, on earth with me; and he was crying for his mommy!

It felt as though my heart was ripping out of my chest and following my son to the next room. I wanted so badly to hold him and be with him, but the doctors had explained I wouldn't be able to hold him for some time. I could touch him and caress him, but he would need to be in the NICU for a couple of months—or at least until he was bigger.

It seemed like the delivery had taken hours. My perception of time stopped during the procedure. I had been concentrating so hard on breathing and not vomiting that I felt as though I had been in there for ages. In reality, it had only been about an hour.

The main doctor said, "We're doing a tubal ligation, right?"

"A what? What is that?" I asked.

"Getting your tubes tied," he said.

I hesitated. Later, I would find out from my husband that I only hesitated for a few seconds, but it felt like several minutes until I answered him.

"Yes, that's right," I said.

He must have been aware of my momentary lapse, because he said to me, "You know you need to have this done. You really shouldn't try to have more children—it could be the end of you."

Chas took over and told him to go through with it. I knew it was the right thing to do, but I still had the nagging feeling that I was being pressured into something unnecessary. It had taken me this long to get pregnant; chances were I couldn't again, so why tie my tubes? I felt I had no choice, so I continued to endure fifteen more minutes of what I thought was sheer torture. *Amazing,* I thought, *only fifteen minutes for a woman to go from having the privilege of bearing children to stopping that option altogether.*

After the procedure, I could tell Chas was getting antsy and I realized he wanted to go see his son, so I told him to go see Connor.

"Are you sure? Don't you want me to stay with you?"

"Mom can take care of me. Just go see our son. Let me know how he's doing," I said.

Mom stayed with me while they put me back in my room to recover. Once I was there and settled, Chas came in. I was surprised to see him already, but apparently it had been over half an hour. Time, it seems, was still playing tricks on my mind.

He walked into the room, leaned over and kissed my forehead, opened his phone, and said, "Meet your son, sweetie."

On his phone was a thirty-second video clip of Connor. The tubes in his mouth were for feeding only, because he was breathing well and very strong, especially considering he was only one pound five ounces. I wanted to jump out of my bed. Tears of joy streamed down my face as I played the video over and over again.

Chas was calm and level-headed as he most always is, but I could tell he was proud. He described to me how tiny Connor was and how he sounded like a little kitten—just like he did when he was first born.

We arranged to have Chas take my mother to the NICU so she could see her newest grandchild and I was left alone in my room. The quietness was almost deafening. So much had been going on around me the last few days, I hadn't realized how crazy it had been in that tiny, suffocating room. Now that I had it all to myself, I was almost scared. I wanted to be with my son—I wanted to hold him—I wanted to be normal again so I could take care of him.

As the room seemed to close in on me, I fell asleep. I hadn't realized I had been sleeping until hours later when the nurses began moving me to a different room. I would be much closer to Connor and it was bigger and more comfortable. I wanted to go see Connor, but everybody kept telling me I had to wait until I was stable.

"Stable? I feel fine. I feel better than I have in days. I want to go see my son," I said to the nurses.

One nurse said, "You have been through a lot the last little while. You need to rest so you can be strong for your son."

After much discussion, I realized they were right. I wanted to be a good mother and I wanted to be able to take care of Connor—and my family. I agreed to get some more sleep and see him the next day.

Alyssa was able to drive down with family members so she could see her new little brother. Kids under fourteen years of age were not allowed in the NICU, so only Alyssa and my stepdaughters, Heather and Shantae, would get to see him. The others would have to wait until he left the hospital. Thankfully, we had plenty of video and cameras to show off, so everybody would get to see him in some way.

## *Sweet Child of Mine*

Welcome, little one.
Your mommy and daddy love you so.

"Hello my precious child,"
I said as I saw your face.
I have waited so long
To be here—in this special place.

To finally be with you,
To hold you tightly in my embrace.
The ache of longing is over,
I can feel sweetly of your Grace.

Thank you, dear Lord, for this precious miracle,
Sent to us from your lofty heights above.
We will live each day with strength and desire,
To always give this child all of our love.

Welcome, little one,
Your mommy and daddy love you so.

- Amy C. Maddocks -

CHAPTER TWELVE

# MOM, I HAVE A SON!

Hours later, I woke up to find several people in my room. Relatives had driven down to see the new addition to our family and there were many arrangements to be made. We had to manage me staying in Salt Lake for the next few months while Connor grew stronger. The hospital staff was helpful, and after talking and weighing our options, it was decided that I would be staying at a Ronald McDonald house in downtown Salt Lake. The cost was minimal and I would have a shuttle to and from the hospital so I could be with Connor as much as I wanted. I was actually excited to take a break from life and focus solely on my son.

The nurses ushered everybody out of the room except my mother. Chas was spending all the time he could with Connor, so my mom was taking care of me. The lights in the room were dimmed, giving my surroundings an almost surreal, candlelit appearance.

I looked over at my mother, who was looking back at me with

a look of pride in her eyes, and I whispered, "Mom, I have a son!"

I felt such elation at this pronouncement and words could not express how I felt. But she knew; she had given birth to six children, two girls and four boys. She knew how I had longed for many years for more children. She had a glistening in her eyes as she whispered back to me, "I know, sweetie; you finally have your son."

That moment in time is forever frozen for me. Only a mother can understand what it means to carry a child in your womb and then welcome that child into the world. How unfortunate men cannot know this same feeling of adoration and pride. There were many times that I felt badly my husband could not feel what it means to know you are a host for a living, breathing baby. I was so grateful my mother was there and that she knew exactly what I meant when I said those words. Nothing else needed to be said at that moment. We both knew how special and spiritual it was.

My brothers arrived and we arranged for them to give Connor a priesthood blessing. They were given special permission to enter the NICU and they went with Chas and his brother and gave Connor a name for our church records and a special blessing to give him and his family strength for all that we would be going through.

I was saddened I could not be there to witness such a powerful, precious event. Imagine grown men surrounding a tiny little baby, placing their hands upon his head, and tenderly giving him a blessing sent down from our Father in Heaven. After hearing of the words spoken, I drew strength from his blessing and felt a renewed energy to forge ahead with the weeks of hardship we had facing us.

Finally the moment came when I was given permission to see my son. Chas brought in a wheelchair and they unhooked my IV from the main machine so I could maneuver. I swung my legs to the side of the bed and put some weight on them. It was reassuring to have my strength back after the episode from the night before.

I sat down in the wheelchair and noticed a weird feeling where my staples were. All of a sudden there was a warm, tingling sensation. I mentioned it to Chas. We figured it was normal, but he told a nurse at the nurse's station as we rode by. She had me go right back into my room to check me out and, sure enough, my wound was bleeding more than it should have been.

They put me back in the bed and undressed my bandages to see what was going on. I was ordered to stay in bed until they were certain the bleeding was under control.

Oh, the frustration I felt at that moment was intense! I begged and pleaded with the nurse and doctor. I needed to see my baby boy, and I didn't care about my welfare or losing a little blood.

"Can you please just wrap it up tight and let me go see him?" I asked.

The doctor said, "You have already lost a lot of blood and you're back on blood thinners, so no, you really can't get out of bed. In fact, your catheter needs to stay in for another day or two and I want you on total bed rest until we are sure the preeclampsia and bleeding are under control."

I couldn't believe what I was hearing. Chas excused the doctor and thanked him for his help. He could tell I was on the verge of losing control, so he tried to talk to me and calm me. I felt as though I was sitting on a bed of nails—poking me in such a way that I wouldn't be comfortable until I was with my son. I didn't remember this intense feeling of separation when Alyssa was born.

Surrounding me was a layer of emptiness that I felt could only be filled with having Connor with me. I felt as though a part of me was gone—yet it was within my grasp—just down the hall.

Everybody kept telling me to rest and get better so I could be with Connor and take good care of him. Yet, these same people were able to go and see my son, be with him, hear him, smell of his sweet baby smells, and sense his spirit. I was being deprived of these feelings, and I wasn't taking it lightly.

Twice more that day I tried to go see him, and twice more that day my wound started bleeding again.

The night before, when we had gotten settled in my room and dimmed the lights to rest, I had an asthma attack. The doctors feared it was blood clots in my lungs again, so they ordered a scan. When it came back negative, they put me on a breathing treatment and started me back on blood thinners. Now they were wondering if they had started them too soon. My wound wasn't healing like it should have been, and they thought maybe the medications were to blame.

Later on, after everybody had left, the room had stopped spinning, and I had been resting for several hours, I was able to go and see my son.

Chas wheeled me down the room as quickly as he dared. He described the different rooms to me as we went by, pointing out the areas he had been visiting the last couple of days. It was nice to be out where the living world existed. I hadn't realized how closed off I had felt from the real world.

We went into the NICU and started to wash up. Chas explained the washing procedure and why we needed to be sure we were clean. It wasn't required, but I wore a mask around my mouth just in case I had an unseen, unknown germ lurking in my breath. It amazed me that masks weren't required, but things had changed since I had given birth to my other little preemie.

We went past what seemed like endless rows of little babies hooked up to all sorts of machines. It broke my heart to see those tiny souls not wrapped up in their mommies' arms. There were several nurses taking care of the babies, and many doctors, as well. Parents were mingled throughout, helping with the care of their children.

I kept asking where Connor was, until we turned down a row of incubators and went to the very end. Connor's name decorated one of the plastic cradles with teddy bear pictures and puppy dogs. I was speechless—I would get to see my son at last! Chas set me up so I could be raised onto a chair at my son's level, and I was finally able to see him in person.

My emotions got the better of me and I couldn't prevent

myself from crying. Chas was discreetly filming my first visit with my son, and I vaguely heard him ask me something.

"Tears of joy, honey?" he asked.

"No! He's so helpless and I can't hold him. He's so tiny."

"Oh, honey, he's going to be fine. He's a fighter. The nurses and doctors already have nicknames for him. They call him 'Spitfire' and 'Firecracker' because he works so hard to take care of himself. He is breathing on his own but he needs higher levels of oxygen, so they are giving him breathing tubes and he keeps fighting them because he wants to do it on his own." Chas then glanced down at his tiny son and took my hand in his. "They don't want him to expend too much energy, so they are keeping him on the breathing tubes," he said.

I still couldn't stop myself from crying, and a nurse noticed. He came to my side and asked if everything was okay.

"She'll be fine. This is her first time down because every time she tried to come see him she had problems with her staples," Chas told him.

The nurse asked if I had any questions, and all I could do was shake my head. I wanted to be left alone while I talked to my son.

I opened the side door on his incubator and reached my hand inside. It was very warm, and I was grateful he had that comfort. I cupped my hand over his head and said, "Hello, little one. Mommy is here for you."

Then the most amazing thing happened. Connor grimaced and started crying his little meow cry like he did when he was born. He recognized me—I just knew it. He knew his mommy and he was letting me know he missed me. I felt the same kinship with him I had felt when he was inside of me.

It was such a bittersweet moment. On one hand, I was so happy to see my son, yet on the other hand, it was heartbreaking that he was in this predicament. I felt as though his tears and cries were because he wanted to be with me, not cooped up in a plastic cage with tubes poking him everywhere.

Even when Alyssa was born preemie, there wasn't this much heartache. I at least got to hold her and take care of her while she stayed in the hospital. This was different; this time I could only watch helplessly as my son fought for his life with every breath.

I stayed with him for as long as the nurses—and Chas—would let me. When they realized I was hurting and light-headed, they forced me to go back to my room. As Chas pushed me down the hall that time, my surroundings seemed to close in on me. I had never noticed how very drab the halls of a hospital were until then. I was reaching out for something to brighten my mood, and everything seemed a dull gray. Even the signs hung on the walls announcing events and such were just plain white.

That wheelchair ride was a long one. I felt like my hospital bed was the furthest thing away from my child. Then I felt anger and frustration. My body was not allowing me to stay with my son, who needed me more than anything. I knew the nurses and doctors were taking good care of him, but only I could give him the calming presence of his mother. Only I could help him fight through all this with my passion and courage.

When Chas got me into the lonely room and helped me into bed, I curled up into a ball and wept. He could only stand by and caress my hair and back while he watched helplessly. There was nothing he could do, either.

"Please go be with him," I said. "He needs strength, and I can't be there. Please go spend time with him and let him know how much you love him."

Chas said, "Are you sure? I need to take care of you, too."

"I'm going to be fine. I just need time to heal. Go and spend as much time as you can with him. I'll be fine, and I can send a nurse to get you if I need anything."

So he went to be with our son—when I couldn't. The only thing I could do was to get better as quickly as possible.

My nurse came in to give me my pain meds, dimmed the lights in my dreary room, and I quickly fell asleep. I had peaceful dreams of playing with my son in the spring grass, wading with him in our backyard pond, and making snowmen with him in the winter snow. I was finally going to have my sweet son.

*Our greatest glory*
*is not in never failing*
*but in rising*
*every time we fall.*

- Confucius -

## CHAPTER THIRTEEN

# TROUBLE BEGINS

I was able to go and visit Connor several more times over the next day. Each visit was so sweet. He was doing well and getting stronger every hour. The nurses and doctors said the first twenty-four hours were the most critical, and he had made it through them with vigor. I was so proud of his little nicknames, "Spitfire" and "Firecracker." It was perfect that he had arrived on New Year's Eve. He was living up to his names and acting as though he did come in with a bang on a most special night.

Every time I saw my son, he recognized me and my voice. I guess only a parent can know the true joy and rapture to be felt when your tiny little child is so filled with love for you.

The nurses asked me if I wanted to change his diaper, and told me Chas wouldn't. I couldn't understand why until I tried. He was so tiny and fragile that you felt as though he would break with every touch. The nurses tried to explain to us that they really were tougher than they seemed, but it was scary to think I might hurt my child. So after a couple of attempts, I decided it was best to let the professionals handle it. I could still touch him, caress him, talk to him, and love him—but the daily care he needed would have to come from me later on when he was stronger.

Each morning the staff in the NICU got together to review each baby's information and progress. Parents were welcome to attend these meetings, so Chas went to them. On the morning of January 2$^{nd}$, he came back with some frightening news. Connor was not breathing as well as he should be, so they had to put him on a ventilator. He also had a valve in his heart that was supposed to close, but since he was born so early, it hadn't formed completely. They were giving him medications that would hopefully speed up the development, but if it didn't work he would need surgery. To top things off, he had gotten an infection in his lungs. They were giving him antibiotics and keeping a close watch, but it was going to be tough for him.

Chas was worried about telling me all this because he didn't want to upset me. But I needed to know what trials we were going to face and I had to be strong for Connor. Plus, these things were normal for preemies. They had more obstacles to go through and this was just a part of those challenges.

Different family members were able to come and see us that day, including Alyssa and Heather, Chas's oldest daughter. It was wonderful for them to go and see Connor. They couldn't get over how tiny he was—and yet how strong. He was a little fighter and it showed.

Later that day a doctor came in to check my C-section wound. She discovered there was some blood pooling underneath the staples and sent for another doctor to confirm what she was noticing. A few hours later he arrived and confirmed the same thing. He removed a few of the staples to see what was going on, and there was some internal bleeding. He found a couple of blood vessels that were not closing and tied them off to keep them from bleeding. Then he left those few staples off so he could check on me later and make sure everything was healing. This meant I could not go and be with Connor for a few hours.

I hunkered down for a long afternoon and Chas went to be with him. The nurses kept a close watch on me and I got some needed rest. A little while later, one of the nurses went to check on my wound, and she got a look of shock on her face as she pulled back the dressings. She called in a few more nurses and told me there was some bleeding and she just needed some help to control it. I looked down and not only was my stomach covered in blood, but so was my bed. I could tell she was trying to keep her cool for my sake, so I tried not to freak out—but it was a lot of blood. She applied pressure to my wound, called the doctor, and sent for Chas.

When Chas walked in and blinked his eyes several times while squinting, I knew it wasn't good. They had laid my bed back so I was flat, which meant I wasn't able to see anything. That was a good thing, because I don't do too well with blood—especially my own. The nurses were applying a lot of pressure, so they increased my pain meds while waiting for the doctor to arrive.

Chas held my hand and tried to reassure me everything was going to be okay. Connor was doing well at the moment, although he still had that infection in his lungs, so Chas stayed with me while they tried to control the bleeding.

An hour later the doctor arrived. I had lost a lot of blood and was light headed, and after evaluating the wound, he decided I needed to go back into surgery. They would have to put me under this time, because they were going to have to cauterize the wound completely. I had several new vessels that were bleeding, including arterial ones, so tying them off wasn't going to work this time.

They arranged for emergency surgery while Chas and I discussed what was going to happen. Surgery is always a nightmare for me—in fact it takes me several weeks just to recover from the effects of anesthesia. I gave explicit instructions to him that I was to be awakened as soon as possible. I didn't have the luxury of taking my time recovering and healing. I had to be with my son—especially while he was fighting multiple problems.

*No one saves us but ourselves.*
*No one can*
*and no one may.*
*We ourselves must walk the path.*

- BUDDHA -

## CHAPTER FOURTEEN

# FAITH FALTERS

I awoke from my surgery in a fog. I couldn't place where I was or what I was doing. I was in a dimmed room; my mother was in one corner and my husband in another. Both of them looked exhausted and worn out. I mumbled something and both of them immediately came to my side.

"How is Connor doing?" I asked groggily.

"He's doing well. I was just with him and he's sleeping right now, but breathing fine and being a little fighter," Chas said.

I asked if I could please go and see him. The nurse came in and started working on my IV. I asked again if I could go and see Connor, and Chas told me I could soon. The next thing I realized, I had fallen asleep again and woke to my mother reading by my side.

"Can I go see Connor now?" I asked her.

"Yes, dear. Let's get you a little more awake and we'll get you down there."

"How long has it been since my surgery?" I asked her.

"About five hours, sweetie. I know that's longer than you wanted, but the nurse insisted you get some more rest," she said.

This infuriated me. I felt the room start to close in on me. I felt a strong need to spend every moment possible with him.

I asked my mother to help me up and get the wheelchair prepped for me. I noticed Chas was not in the room and my mother didn't seem to be moving as quickly as I felt she should be.

"Why do you seem so calm, Mom?" I asked her.

"Why shouldn't I be?"

"It just seems like you would be a little more frantic about things, with how Connor is doing and such," I said.

"You know you are all in good hands, and everything is being done that can be. Connor's doing really well. The nurses treat him as if he is their own son, and it makes me feel good that they care so much. But I sure wish they would let me ask questions and see him more," she said.

"I put you on the list of people able to see him, so there shouldn't be any problem with you being in there," I told her.

"I know, dear, but they are still really reserved about how much information they will give me. Whenever I ask something, they look at Chas to make sure he's okay with them discussing things with me. They are so protective, and I would have thought grandparents would have access to the same information as parents."

We talked for a while about the different laws put in place for the privacy of patients. I realized this was doing me a lot of good because I was fighting going back to sleep. I was finally able to ask how my surgery went, and she told me it went well. They opened the original C-section wound back up completely and cauterized everything so I wasn't bleeding anymore. They were going to start giving me blood because I had lost so much, but they decided I would be okay once they had stopped the bleeding.

The biggest problem was that they had to leave the wound open. They didn't want to close it up because the blood thinners I was on wouldn't allow it to heal properly. So they left it open and just bandaged me up. It was painful, but nothing unbearable. More painful was not being with my son.

Again, the room started to close in on me and I felt a pressure from the darkened walls pushing down upon me like a collapsing accordion. I needed to get out of this suffocating room and go be with my son.

My mother had to leave to go back home and take care of the rest of the family and work, so we said our goodbyes after Chas came back to take me down to see Connor.

As he wheeled me down the long corridor, he updated me on how our son was doing.

"He is such a little fighter, hon! I'm so proud of him. It's like he just keeps striving to be strong and acts like he's a full term baby, ready to be with his parents."

Connor's stats were all back to normal and he looked so pink and beautiful when Chas wheeled me around the corner. All I saw was my little baby. Nobody and nothing else was around us. I could see him moving around and fighting the nurse every time she tried to take blood or move his cords around. I could *feel* his love for me, even through the Plexiglas covers of his incubator.

I found it interesting how such a tiny little thing can wrap your entire existence around his one little finger and you are hooked for eternity. Only he existed in my world at that moment, and I was so grateful to just be in his presence. For such a small little guy, he emitted a huge aura of love and peace. I silently said a prayer to my Father in Heaven to please watch over and protect my son. I asked only that He help him to fight his prematurity and grow quickly. *Not too much to ask, right?* I thought to myself.

I laughed inwardly, because I began to have that same feeling of being in a movie. All else around me ceased to exist. Connor and I were the only two people in the world at that moment. All of the beeps, whirs, and noises from the other babies and their machines slowly faded into nothing. Connor and I were together again—the aching feeling I had felt since he left my womb receded and I felt whole again. Touching this precious body, feeling this special soul sent down to me from Heaven above, I realized what a true miracle life really is. Forget science—this perfect being in front of me was proof that God was real and He trusted me to take care of this spirit.

Examining his body, it was amazing to me that I could pick out similarities between Chas and me. He had his daddy's big nose, which was good because they had to put tubes of oxygen in them and this allowed for plenty of room. He had my stubby chin and chunky toes. It was so hard to believe that at just less than two pounds you could still tell he was our son. I was also amazed at how much hair he had. Had he gone full term, he would have had a head full of hair. It was dark brown with a slight curl, just like his daddy's.

The next few hours were sweet and treasured. I attempted to change his diaper, making fun of Chas because he didn't dare. Yet when I tried to do it I understood why Chas couldn't. He was so tiny and his skin so soft I felt like I was going to break him or rip his flesh. So I helped the nurse do it and did the best I could. He loved every touch and caress we gave him. The expressions on his face confirmed he knew who his parents were, especially when I talked to him. He responded to my voice the way he would have if he had known me for a hundred years. Whenever the nurse had to move him around for something, he would flail his arms and legs while grimacing, yet when Chas or I touched him, he seemed to smile and coo.

We took lots of video of him and hundreds of pictures. The nurses had also been taking pictures and even made a CD of them. Each time they took pictures, they put them all on the same CD for us to take home when we took our baby home with us.

At one point during the enjoyable hours we spent taking care of our baby, his stats went down. He wasn't getting enough oxygen—even with the respirator. It was very frightening to be there while the nurses and doctors scrambled to get Connor back to a stable condition, watching in the sidelines while not being able to do anything. It took what seemed like hours to get him to a point where the doctors thought he was stable again, but in reality, it was only around fifteen minutes.

I stayed by his side until I was in intense pain from the surgery and practically falling over from exhaustion. Late past the midnight hour, Chas and the nurses convinced me to go back and get some needed sleep and something to eat. They assured us Connor was doing very well and they would let us know right away if anything changed, but our son also needed his rest.

We went to the cafeteria together and picked out some food to take back up to my room. It was the first time in days I felt confident and at peace. Chas and I had a chance to talk, laugh, and have fun together in that cafeteria. It was full of a huge variety of foods and workers ready to help—even in the wee hours of the morning. I was becoming more and more impressed with this hospital as time went by.

We left our food there while Chas wheeled me back up to my room. The plan was for him to get me tucked in and then he'd return to get our food. It was too difficult to wheel a chair around and hold two trays at the same time.

I got into bed excited to have food. I couldn't remember the last time I had eaten, and I had been on such a strict diet before that I was excited to eat a simple sandwich.

I played over the events of the day in my mind while waiting for Chas to return, and the one thing that kept recurring was, *Why was the Lord putting us through this trial? Why couldn't I just have children like the majority of mothers did, full term—healthy babies?* I loved being pregnant, and yet I did it so poorly. Other women hated being pregnant and yet they delivered healthy babies that didn't have to struggle as mine did.

What had I done to deserve this? Was the Lord punishing me for something? I always believed God wouldn't punish us for anything, and that everything we went through was to make us stronger and more faithful. I decided my mind was just torturing me and playing tricks —I was never one to question God's will, so I put a stop to it almost as fast as those thoughts started.

Yet, as I lay there for a few moments alone, I couldn't help but wonder why Connor had to suffer so. Punish *me*—not him. He was an innocent little baby, and yet he had to fight for his every breath.

I told myself I had to focus on the positive, keep my attitude up, and just worry about how to help Connor, not hinder him. I finally had my baby boy—my life was complete. I had to be the very best mother I could be.

A feeling of peace and comfort washed over me like a warm shower. I knew the Lord was giving me the comfort and confirmation I needed. Something whispered in my mind that everything would be okay—regardless of what was to come, everything would be all right.

I settled into my bed, turned on the TV, and as I heaved a sigh of relief and contentment, a NICU nurse came running into my room at full speed with another nurse behind her, pushing a wheel chair.

"You need to come with us—now," she said with a tone of authority and urgency.

Another nurse followed right behind, clipped my IV off, yanked it out of the machine, and started pulling me to my feet all in one movement. I was startled and confused.

"Connor's not doing well," the NICU nurse said, "I don't know if he'll make it and you need to be with him right now."

"What?" I yelled and questioned with the same word.

"There is no time for talking right now. You'll find out more when we get there. Someone has already been sent down to get your husband from the cafeteria. Please just stay strong right now, for you and your son." She ran with my wheelchair as fast as she dared push it down the hallways and around corners.

My heart pounded out of my chest. I couldn't catch my breath, my hands were shaking as though the temperature had plummeted, and my entire soul screamed in denial. *This wasn't happening! This is all a bad, horrible nightmare and I'm going to wake up any second now! Wake up, Amy!*

It was during the fastest wheel chair ride I had ever been on, and the slowest, that I realized *I'm not dreaming—my son could die. This is a nightmare playing out in real life.*

*Take back that sad word goodbye;*
*bring back the joy to my life.*
*Don't leave me here with these tears,*
*come and kiss the pain away.*
*I can't forget the day you left,*
*time is so unkind,*
*and life is so cruel without you here beside me.*

- Lyrics to "Unbreak My Heart"
as sung by Toni Braxton -

## CHAPTER FIFTEEN

# PRECIOUS MOMENTS

As we flew past the washing station I wondered why we weren't washing up. Normally, every time you go into the NICU, you are required to scrub your hands and arms for a good five to ten minutes. Now the nurses were whooshing me past the sinks as if they didn't exist. My mind said, *hey—we need to wash up!* Yet my rational side said it didn't matter when they thought no amount of cleanliness could save your child.

As we turned the last corner to the aisle where Connor was, awareness slapped me in the face. I first saw Chas, towering above everybody else as he usually does with his six-foot-three inch frame, and he held Connor's hand while talking gently to him. I heard urgency in his voice as it cracked with despair. Then I saw several doctors and nurses surrounding Connor, who wasn't in his incubator. The sides of it had been turned down so he was exposed to everything around him. I got defensive, thinking they were putting his life in further danger by exposing him to the elements. Later I realized they had to do so as a last-ditch resort to try and help him live while they had easier access to him.

The team of care givers parted to allow room for me to pull a stool up to Connor's side. I didn't have to ask what was going on—the looks on their faces told me enough. One nurse had a large bag attached to a tube in Connor's mouth and she was quickly squeezing it to give him the air he couldn't get himself. Chas had tears in his eyes as he told me Connor's stats had gone down and this time they weren't coming back up. Even with all the machines, technology, and high IQ's in the room, nothing was going to save my baby. The only thing left was a miracle from God.

Chas and I both talked to Connor, and the doctors said to keep it up. One of them said it would help him to know his parents were there. We prayed—inwardly and openly—while we let the team work on keeping him alive. At one point, when several nurses had taken turns squeezing the bag, the doctors stepped back and stopped his air. Connor was breathing on his own, but he wasn't getting enough oxygen to stay alive.

They quietly gave us room while we looked at each other in confusion. Chas seemed to be more coherent than I was, because I looked around and started panicking.

"Honey, why aren't they working on him anymore? He's still alive!"

With tears in his eyes, he looked at me and then slowly turned toward the team standing a few feet away from us. He whispered, "Why can't you save him?"

I watched as one of the nurses looked at the head doctor with pleading in her eyes. The doctor seemed to give in as she nodded her head once and her shoulders sagged. With that gesture, the nurse stepped forward and started squeezing the bag as much as her tired arms would allow.

Then the doctor came a little closer to us and told us in as simple terms as possible that our son would not survive the night. He had been through so much already for such a small baby, and in the process of trying valiantly to keep him alive, his lungs had been hammered and used up. "If" he could survive, he would never be able to breathe on his own and he would have multiple problems.

I didn't care. It didn't matter to me what tomorrow would bring. I was only concerned about the here and now—and I wanted my son. I felt as though they were giving up on him. I begged and pleaded with God to please spare his life. I was having multiple problems as well—why couldn't my life be taken for his? He had only been on this earth for three short days; surely the Lord would see fit to give him a life here?

After what seemed like hours, the doctors and nurses cried along with Chas and me as we sobbed and tried to reason with God. Chas did his best to be strong for me, yet I could see in his eyes and hear in his voice the torment and the pain wracking his soul.

My sweet, strong husband, who never cried, never lost control, and rarely showed emotion other than to tease, was cowering like a lost child as he tried to hold me and caress our son—all the while trying to come to terms with the fact that Connor's life was slowly fading away.

"Why? Why? Why?" I shouted to anyone that would listen. "This isn't happening," I said as I slowly shook my head side to side. I knew I was being irrational and I looked like an idiot, but I couldn't believe my son was dying.

The nurses asked me, through tears of their own, if I would like to hold him before he died. I couldn't talk or communicate at that point, so through my sobbing, I nodded yes.

They unhooked him from the machines and Chas helped them gently pick him up and place him in my arms as though he was a fragile piece of glass. To see my husband handing me our son, knowing full well this would be the only time I would get to hold him alive, was just too much. I started to collapse just as Chas and the nurses realized what was happening. They managed to get me to a sitting position and help me hold Connor while I tried to focus. I had to pull myself together for the moment—for I didn't know how long the moment would last.

With every ounce of energy and will I had left, I held my long-awaited son while I covered him with my kisses and tears. I talked to him as only I knew how—letting him know how very much I loved him and how proud of him I was for his fight to stay alive—even if it was for only a short time.

I looked up at Chas and realized how selfish I was being. He had been by Connor's side more than I had these last few days, and here I was taking up what few precious moments we had left with him.

"Would you like to hold your son?" I asked him through misty eyes, puffy nose, and mumbling lips.

"Thank you, dear," he whispered back as he took our sweet son into his arms. Chas' eyes were red with both tears and fury. The look of utter exhaustion and pain on his face broke what little there was left of my shattered heart. As he stood above me holding our son, he could only caress Connor's little face and tell him how much he loved him. I heard him say, "I was going to be a good daddy for you, Connor. I was going to teach you everything I know."

A nurse approached us then, and I realized we weren't alone for the first time in what seemed like hours—yet only minutes as well. Suddenly I looked around and there were at least ten different nurses and doctors standing close by. Not one of them had dry eyes. Everyone was touched by the serene atmosphere surrounding us. The nurse asked us if we would like to be alone with Connor, and we both nodded. They got me back into my wheelchair and Chas handed me my baby. Then he wheeled me down the hallway and into a little room that looked like a lounge. They gave me Connor's blanket to wrap him in and Chas and I sat next to each other, both of us holding our little "Firecracker" while he took what would be his last breaths.

The next hour was like having the ultimate paradise within your grasp and then having to let that perfect serenity go, realizing you held in your hands a prized and innocent soul that had to be given back to God. We spent every moment with Connor loving him as best we could, and holding each other while we cried for our lost future. Our hopes, dreams, and desires were fading away with each last breath Connor took. When the doctor came in and could no longer hear a heartbeat, she called the time of death.

Our son, who came into this world on December 31, 2006, like a little firecracker, left us with a gaping hole in our hearts at 7:14 a.m. on January 3, 2007. Three short, wonderful, bittersweet days that could never be replaced or removed from memory.

## *Remembrance*

*Tears fall from my eyes*
*as softly the memories flow,*
*with the tears, salty on my tongue.*
*I miss you so much.*

*Tomorrow is frightening*
*except for the thought*
*of seeing you again;*
*another time, another place.*

*I hear your voice...*
*in my dreams you come.*
*We talk and laugh*
*about silly, important things.*

*Each day without you is less;*
*less bright, less full, ...less.*
*I feel your love with me,*
*yet, I want you to hold.*

*Faith in God eases the pain*
*for moments, sometimes days.*
*Still, I cry; but not for you,*
*for the loss I feel in me.*

- Brenda Penepent -

## CHAPTER SIXTEEN

# SHOCK AND DENIAL

We were told we could keep Connor with us for twenty-four hours, and then we had to turn him over to the coroner for a time. We refused an autopsy after talking with the doctors and knowing we didn't want his precious little body invaded. We knew what had killed him, so there was no need.

Chas wheeled me back to my room while I held my baby, just like any other mother in that hospital. Only I wasn't like anyone else there—my son was dead.

As we settled into my room, a ringing of chimes came across the loud speaker. In days past, each time we heard those chimes we giggled with excitement—they meant another baby had been born. Now, the chimes were a death toll bearing down upon us. With grief settling in like a fog covering the beaches in the evening, we both cringed as the sound of a new mother and father's joy came to life. Never before had I felt such raw negative emotions directed at a stranger. *My son is dead*—I wanted to yell—*quit cheering and being so happy!*

I lay down in my hospital bed, snuggled my son next to me under the covers, and watched his little face. I was hoping against hope that he would suddenly start breathing again. My nurse came in to the room and gave me more pain meds—as if medicine could take away this horrible feeling, but within minutes I feel asleep, cradling my little boy.

A couple of hours later, I groggily awoke to find Connor snuggled in my embrace and Chas asleep uncomfortably on a chair. As I came to my senses, I realized like a slap in the face why Connor was next to me instead of down the hall in the NICU. I was instantly nauseous and light-headed. My son was dead. I was lying in a hospital bed holding him, and I didn't have much time before the twenty-four hours was up.

I tried to wake Chas, but the last week had taken its toll on him. *He's sleeping like the dead,* I thought to myself. I realized that term was so inconceivably wrong to think of at that time, and I broke down bawling again. My nurse came running in my room to see if she could help me in any way, but when she saw me holding my son as though he were alive—rocking him gently as if he needed to be soothed—she knew there was nothing anybody could do for me. With her eyes starting to fill with tears, she quietly backed out of the room and closed the door on a scene no one should ever have to witness.

The rest of the day was a blur. After hours of trying to come to terms with the fact that my baby was dead, I finally built up the nerve to let our family know. Alyssa was in school, so calling her was out of the question; if I talked to my mom I would lose control again, so the only logical person to call was my oldest brother, Tony.

Tony is the unofficial "head" of our family since Dad died. He was also a sergeant with the Sheriff's department, so I figured he would keep a level tone with me and make it easy on me to talk about Connor. I reluctantly dialed his number, and when he answered, it took me a moment to speak.

"Hi Tony, it's Amy." I had to gather my breath for the next sentence. "Connor is dead. He died early this morning. They say he got an infection in his lungs and he just couldn't fight it anymore. I need you to tell Alyssa for me, because I don't think I can right now. Please don't call her—tell her in person. And I also need you to let Mom and everyone else know."

I spit it out as fast as the words could come. Tony paused for a moment, and then said, "Oh, sis, I'm so sorry. But, be grateful he doesn't have to put up with this disgusting world."

"I know, I know. So can you tell everyone for me? I just can't call anyone else right now," I asked him through my tears. He told me not to worry and he would take care of everything.

I hung up the phone, thinking what a stupid comment he'd just made. He had a perfectly healthy daughter and son—what right did he have to insinuate this was for the best? I was appalled and upset, but I knew what he said was true. All my brothers are really good at telling things like they are, without sweetening it. Tony, being in law enforcement, saw the ugly side of everything. So it was true, I could be grateful Connor wouldn't have to deal with the ugly things in this world. But that didn't make the pain any easier to cope with. I still wanted my son alive.

Chas woke up and held Connor for a time. How bittersweet it was for us to hold our dear son and touch his perfect features knowing his soul was not with us. Every time I looked at him I thought he looked so normal, and that he just needed to wake up. I kept him tightly wrapped in his blanket and held him close. What else could I do?

Chas started calling his family members. They lived close to the hospital, and they were able to come and visit. There were so many visitors that day, it's still a blur. People came and went, giving their condolences, holding and touching my son, and crying tears of pain that only someone related to the situation could cry. After all, Chas was the baby of the family, and he had lost his only son. As we all knew, life just wasn't fair and it was being made clear to us that day that we were in for a whole new future as unpredictable as the weather.

A few hours after I called Tony, my mom came into the room. There was what seemed like twenty people in my room when I looked up and saw her standing in the doorway, focusing only on me. She told me later I looked like a deer caught in the headlights and her heart broke twice that day—once for the loss of her grandson, and once for the suffering her daughter was going through. She felt the pain of our loss in a whole different way than the rest of the family.

She came immediately to my bed and hugged me while I sobbed again; enormous waves of grief flooding through me as my mom held me tight. My mother had six healthy children, but she also had three miscarriages, and the pain of losing those children came to the surface once again as she lived through the pain of losing a grandson. Although this pain was different, it was still intense and cruel.

She asked me where Connor was and before she could finish her sentence I could see her appalled look of disgust as she saw everybody taking turns holding him. I have learned that everybody grieves differently at the loss of a child, and one thing that may be acceptable and necessary for some, may seem disgraceful and desecrating to others. I knew in that one look my mother did not approve of everybody handling her grandson. She didn't say anything, but she didn't need to. Chas noticed she was there and came over to hug her for a moment. He asked if she would like to hold Connor, and she said she would wait.

After a while, the crowd started to disperse. I saw Chas handing our son over to my mom, who then left the room. He came back and told me he arranged with the nurses for my mother to have some alone time with Connor. I thanked him for that, not knowing how much it would really mean to her, but knowing she needed that time.

After a while, my mother came back. I think she deliberately waited until most everyone had left. She told me later she felt like it just wasn't right to be passing around Connor like he was still alive, and that it was degrading to him. I understood what she meant, but I was also in a state of shock and denial. My mind wasn't as sharp as it usually was, but I at least recognized that those who wanted to hold Connor just needed to vent their own grief, and I needed to let them do so.

My mom had to drive back that night, so she left earlier than I wanted her to. However, it was getting close to the twenty-four hour mark, and the nurses reminded us we would have to turn Connor over to them soon. Chas and I spent our last few moments with him, and then called a nurse in to come get him. When she came, I asked where she would be taking him.

"His body needs to spend the night in the morgue, sweetie, and you can have him back with you in the morning," she said. I was surprised at how easily she stated those facts. I kept focusing on the words "his body," and my heart kept trying to tell me he was still maybe alive, but my mind won over reason and I asked if I could bring him down. She said that was fine, so Chas got the wheelchair and the two of us walked down the long hallways with our son snuggled into my embrace. We had to be escorted by a security guard down to the lower levels of the hospital, and when we got to the door marked "Morgue," I started having trouble breathing.

"I can't go in there, Chas," I cried while holding Connor protectively.

"I'll take him from here, if you'd like," said the nurse who had been walking behind us the whole way.

Chas gently took him from my arms as I kissed his unusually chubby cheeks and told the nurse he would take him, but he would appreciate it if she would wait there with me.

The guard led Chas into the room and I just sat in the dark hallway and sniffed my tears back. The nurse tried to make small talk, but I couldn't respond. She finally gave up and just let me have my moment crying—again.

Chas came out of the room looking five years older. His shoulders were slumped and he looked defeated. We walked back to my room in silence. When we got there, I started asking ridiculous questions. I wondered if they would keep him covered with his blankets, whether or not it would be dark in there, if someone would be with him—all the things that would matter if he were alive.

Chas looked at me with an expression of terror. I realized he was wondering if I had completely lost my mind. I did temporarily lose my mind, and sometimes I wonder if I ever got it back whole. But he was right on one part; I would never be the same—still the same "Amy," but a piece of me was gone—and won't be whole again until I am with my son once more.

The nurse came in and injected a sleep aid into my IV, knowing full well I would not be able to sleep that night without some assistance.

What should have been my son's fourth night on this earth was what I considered to be my first night in hell. For without Connor, what good was life?

*Is it possible, tell me, to hold onto dreams*
*When they've crumbled to ashes, and nothing it seems*
*Remains but the memories of happier days*
*When tomorrow held promise in infinite ways.*

*Can you hold onto hope after losing a child?*
*When nothing makes sense, and nothing's worthwhile?*
*When the days and the nights all roll into one,*
*and though moving's an effort, it's easy to run...*

*But no matter how fast there appears no escape*
*From the pain and heartache that follow and shape*
*the efforts we make to hold onto our dreams...*
*That have crumbled to ashes, that are haunted it seems*
*by our constant companions of guilt and despair;*
*horror and grief tag along everywhere.*

*Where are our answers, where does pain end?*
*I search and I suffer - I ask you again*
*Can you hold onto hope after losing a child?*
*When nothing makes sense, and nothing's worthwhile?*

- Sally Migliaccio -

CHAPTER SEVENTEEN

# Whirlpools of Despair

After a night of continually tossing and turning, being woken up every hour to have my vital signs checked, and crying non-stop about Connor, I gave up on sleep and tried to focus my blurry mind on what needed to be done.

My first decision was to do whatever was necessary to get out of the hospital. It no longer held the loving joy for me that it had before. Everything was a constant reminder that I wouldn't be going home with my baby, and I had to get out quickly.

The first doctor I spoke with told me there was no way I would be going home anytime soon. My wound from the second surgery was still too precarious and I was in no physical condition to take care of myself. He said I needed at least a week in the hospital.

I looked him straight in the eye. "I have a funeral to arrange for my son and I am *not* going to do it from the hospital bed where I should be enjoying his company rather than arranging for his burial. I don't care if I have to get up, rip this IV out of my arm, and walk out those doors, *I will do it*. You can either assist me to make this as easy as possible, or you can back off and watch it happen. You choose."

The doctor must have been shocked because he was speechless. I remember thinking, *How can he be so stupid*?

He finally spoke and said he would see what he could do, but there would have to be preparations made. I agreed and asked him to send the nurse on his way out.

I didn't mean to be rude or disrespectful, but I also was not willing to sit around healing in that hospital. I knew going home without Connor was going to be another trial to bear, but I could not fathom the idea of spending any more time in that hospital. It was supposed to be the place that brought me great joy.

I had actually been looking forward to the arrangements we had made for me to stay in Salt Lake, because it would have allowed me to just be Connor's mommy for a time. That had all been ripped away from me and I desperately wanted to remove myself from this domain of misery and get somewhere where I could focus.

The nurse came in and had the common sense not to ask how I was doing. Instead, she came to my bedside and asked, "Would you like me to bring your son in to be with you?"

*Finally*, I thought, *someone who knows what I need*. "Yes, please. And please take this food tray away. They must have brought it in while I was sleeping and I'm just not hungry."

"Amy, you need to keep your strength up. You really should eat."

"Food is the last thing on my mind right now, I would probably throw it up if I tried it anyway, and it's not like I don't have a few fat cells on reserve. I'll be fine." She nodded her head in understanding and took it away.

She returned a few minutes later with my precious son wrapped up in his blankets, laying him gently in a portable crib. An outsider looking in would not have known that crib carried a dead child. I mentally thanked her for that—she seemed to know I needed to be as much of a mother right then as I could be.

I took my son out of his crib and held him close. He looked the same, but he was cold. No matter how much I rubbed his skin or wrapped him in my warmth, he was not going to magically start breathing and get warm. At that moment, looking at my dead son, realizing my little miracle was gone, I did something I had never done nor would ever even *think* of doing. I cursed God.

I swore to never pray to Him again, pay Him homage, or sing His praises as I had done my entire life. He had taken my son away from me, and selfish as it seemed, I had to blame someone.

I instantly felt blasphemous, but I refused to retract my thoughts. My body had failed Connor and I knew he would be alive and inside my womb right then if my body had been a better incubator for him, but ultimately I felt it was God's fault for taking him from me. He is omnipotent and all-powerful; if He had chosen to let Connor live—he would have.

Chas woke up and looked straight at me, holding our son. The pain in those eyes was unbearable. I had failed my husband, too. He came to my side and held my hand while he caressed our son's tiny face. Then he said to me, "I was going to be such a good daddy. I was even going to impress you with my diaper-changing skills. I was going to show you how much a father can do for a baby and make you so proud of me."

I started sobbing uncontrollably, continually saying, "I'm sorry! I'm sorry!" Chas realized I was trying to apologize for Connor dying and for taking those moments away from him, and he tried to rectify the situation. But nothing he could say or do was going to take away my responsibility for losing our child. I would place that blame on myself and the Lord.

We talked about what needed to be done, and Chas left in order to take care of paperwork. His oldest daughter, Heather, showed up to help us with things and I was grateful she would be with him. Connor was her only brother and she felt his loss already. She and Chas went to get Connor's birth certificate and then make arrangements to transport his body home. We could take him with us if a funeral home approved the transfer, and if we delivered his body to the home that would be doing the service.

The nurses placed a picture of a leaf with raindrops gently falling from its tip on my door. This was the "sign" for a loss in the hospital, and anyone entering my room was supposed to recognize the sign and be gentle.

However, not everyone knew what the picture meant, and it was more heartbreaking to have to explain my child was dead than I had realized. At one point, a little old lady knocked on my door and walked in with flowers and a cheery expression on her face.

"Hello dear. I'm with the local Relief Society of our church, and I wanted to come and see if there was anything we could do for you and your baby," she said jubilantly.

I started crying, as I was doing so much these days, and through broken tears told her my baby had died.

The look of shock and horror on her face is forever etched in my mind. Not everybody can deal with the death of others very well, and the death of a child is so different, and more intense. She started backing out of my room as though suddenly realizing I had a horrible disease. With the flowers still in her hand, she reached blindly behind her with the other and tried to find the doorknob.

"I'm so sorry," was all she had time to blurt out as she found the door and ran quicker than a woman that age should be able to run.

I didn't blame her for her reaction, and I realized I was going to have to get used to it. I would learn the hard way over the next few months that dead children are a taboo subject. Kids were supposed to bury their parents, not vice versa, and a lot of people can't deal with it.

As I lay in my bed alone with my son, I started feeling uncomfortably wet on the front of my shirt. I looked down and realized with horror that my milk had come in. I'd had breast surgery years before, and we were uncertain if I would be able to produce milk. When Connor was just a few hours old, I had been able to get some milk for him, but the nurses had said it usually took a few days, so I had been religiously pumping every few hours since he was born. They were storing what little I had in bottles to be used when he was able to eat. Now nature was playing a cruel trick on me—one that would take months to stop.

I had not used the pump since he died, and yet here was my milk—coming in strong on both sides. When I thought my tears were all used up, I cried some more. *How could the Lord be doing this to me?* As if all of this wasn't hard enough to deal with, now I had to deal with my milk coming in? It was like pouring salt in a wound that keeps growing larger by the hour.

I did what I always do in helpless situations, I called my mother. As I sobbed to her about my milk coming in, she got upset the nurses hadn't prepared me for this. They could have wrapped my breasts with bandages to help with the pain and swelling, and that would hopefully stop the milk from coming in.

She hung up with me and called the nurses' station. A nurse came with some bandages and let me wrap myself as best I could. At that point, I was starting to feel numb with pain. *What else was the Lord going to throw at me?*

As if in answer to my question, I heard a baby start crying in the next room. I had been alone in this wing of the hospital when I was admitted, but now there was a new mother in the room next to me, taking care of her living child. I thought I was going to lose my mind. In response to that, the chimes announcing another new baby started ringing. With each note playing over the intercom, my headache closed in.

I beeped the nurse and told her I needed more pain meds. This was the first time I had asked for them, and she seemed surprised. They had been keeping me on a regular dose since my surgery, and I had been in pain since then, but emotional pain overrides physical pain. I hadn't had a chance to worry about my open wound, but now I thought if they doped me up enough, maybe the mental pain would subside, too.

I was partially right. Once the pain meds kicked in, I seemed to be able to focus better on what needed to be done. I still had phone calls to make, an obituary to write, a burial plot to find, and whatever else comes with a funeral. I was grateful for the meds so I could dull the pain of my son's death, while the woman in the room next to me complained that her baby was crying too much and keeping her awake.

*We think of you in silence*
*And often speak your name,*
*But all that's left to answer*
*Is your picture in a frame.*

*If we could have one lifetime wish*
*One dream that would come true*
*We would pray to God with all our hearts*
*For yesterday and you.*

*If tears could build a stairway*
*And heartaches make a lane*
*We would walk our way to heaven*
*To be with you again.*

- Author Unknown -

CHAPTER EIGHTEEN

# EMPTY HOUSE, EMPTY HEART

Chas was gone most of the day making arrangements, so I did my best to place phone calls and stay as rational as possible. The same thought kept going through my head, *I'm going home without my baby—what am I supposed to do with my life now?*

The nurses opened the blinds in my room, turned the lights up, and made sure the TV was always on. It was their way of trying to "brighten" my mood and help me get through this. All it did was irritate me.

I had no appetite, no desire to even brush my hair. What did those things matter now? My son was lying in my arms—never to move around and cry again—and they were worried about making my room sunny. I couldn't believe the audacity of it all. How could people continue to smile and be happy when my sweet Connor was dead?

Even though I was holding my baby, I felt like a huge chunk

of my soul had left my body. When Connor was no longer inside of me I had immediately felt a severe "aloneness" and a feeling of being incomplete. Now that he was dead, I felt as though I could have pulled my shirt down and seen a gaping hole where my heart used to be. I didn't dare look for fear of what I would find. I needed so badly to hold something tangible—representing my precious child—and yet in some ways it hurt more to hold Connor after his spirit had left his body. He was no longer with me. The unbearable pain in my chest reminded me of that with every breath.

The phone rang and I was startled out of my daze. I didn't want to talk to anyone, but I figured it must have been important, so I picked up the receiver and said hello. It was a dear friend from my church who had offered to arrange for a baby shower for me.

"Hi, Amy, and congratulations! I feel terrible I didn't have your shower before now, but I thought we would have more time. Do you have a minute to talk?" she asked.

Through gut-wrenching tears, I said, "He died; I don't need a shower anymore. I can't talk right now."

Chas and Heather had walked in right when the phone rang. Chas came to my side to take it from my hand. He talked to my friend and briefly explained things while Heather tried to console me.

It's interesting how much water our bodies can produce. I had cried so much in the previous two days that I couldn't believe I had any liquid left to cry out. Yet I did, and I sobbed for a while until I realized Chas was sitting on my bed holding me and rocking me back and forth.

I knew I had to remove myself from the hospital or I would lose my mind completely. Chas arranged for the doctor to come in and we made a deal; if I would eat a few more meals and agree to let home health care nurses come in to re-dress my wound every other day, I could go home.

So I obeyed and ate. Food had never tasted so bland to me. I am not one to complain about hospital food—I always figured it tasted pretty good because I didn't have to prepare it or clean it up. This time it seemed putrid to me, but each bite brought me closer to home, so I kept eating and drinking as much as I could to help convince the doctor I would be good.

Some technicians came in and taught me about the machine that was going to be hooked up to me for a while. They called it a "Wound-Vac" and it did just that. It worked like a continuous vacuum that kept my wound clean and helped it to heal quicker. A piece of foam was cut to fit the size of my wound, shoved inside of it, then a hose was attached to the foam which was then all taped down to make sure of a good seal. The hose then attached to a machine that sucked the infection out and kept the wound clean.

This was supposed to speed up the process of closing my wound, and was also supposed to make things easier for me. I would have to keep the machine attached to me, change the foam and tape bandages every other day, and let a nurse check on me as much as possible. I didn't care—whatever got me out of this horrible place, the better.

My hospital room felt more and more like a public meeting place. People were continually coming in and out checking on me or the wound machine, changing bed linens, cleaning the bathroom, or otherwise stopping by to see the poor wounded mother whose baby had died.

Connor was still with me, wrapped up tightly in his little blanket, always by my side. I felt like a side show freak at a circus. I told Chas I was going to start charging fees for whoever wanted to come in and gawk at me. He talked to the nurses and the steady flow of people seemed to subside. My phone also stopped ringing, so I assumed the nurses were starting to screen my calls as well.

That evening, Chas and I were able to bathe our son, lotion his soft skin, and dress him in cute baby clothes a volunteer had made for the babies in the NICU. We picked out a warm, soft blanket and wrapped him tightly in it. This would be the only time we would get to bathe our son and take care of him, and the nurses took pictures while we did it. They knew we would want those pictures later, and they were right.

Chas and I spent one more lonely night in that room with our son, and the next morning we prepared to leave. Chas cleaned up all of the breast-pump equipment I had used, packed it away in the case it came in, and then dumped the few bottles of milk I had saved for our son down the sink. He took care of everything; and he did it with such valor. The man was like a mountain of steel; never wavering from what had to be done, and yet he was a giant, cuddly teddy bear when I needed him to hold me while I cried. I knew this was just as painful for him as it was for me, yet here he was, taking care of a blithering idiot of a wife, knowing he would be going home without his son.

We were checked out and ready to go when the nurse brought the wheelchair to my room. Impatiently, I listened to all the instructions the doctor had given her, signed the release form as quickly as possible, and then told Chas I was ready to go. He brought the wheelchair to my bed-side and helped me get up.

I hobbled over to it and managed to get comfortable, and then Chas handed our baby to me to take home. For one brief moment—one glistening speck of light peeked through my dark aura—and I felt like a real mother going home with her baby. After all, I *looked* like one, why couldn't I pretend to *be* one?

I wrapped Connor up tightly and Chas started to wheel me down the long hallway. It was snowing outside, so each window we passed was dark and dreary. We went to the elevator with a nurse and got in to go to the lobby floor.

A high, piercing voice cut through the silence when the elevator doors closed. "Oh, what a tiny little baby! I can't see him, but he must be so small. Look at the tiny little baby, dear," a woman said to her little girl.

The girl looked to be around eight-years-old and both she and her mother peered around me to try and take a look at Connor. I instinctively covered him even more and turned my shoulder toward them so they couldn't see. *How could they?* I wondered to myself. *How could they be so thoughtless?*

Some nagging little angel in the deep recesses of my mind tried telling me they didn't know my child was dead. They just saw a mother and father with their baby bundle going out of the hospital. How could they know he was not alive? How common was it to leave the hospital with your baby not breathing?

I ignored the sense of reasoning trying to come forth in my mind and settled on fuming instead. But I wasn't about ready to say to them, "My son is dead; would you like to see?" So I continued being rude while Chas and the nurse kept quiet. The air seemed to be as thick as a humid southern evening in our little elevator, and the ride felt like it was taking us all the way down to hell.

We finally got to the bottom floor and Chas wheeled me out and got me to the car. He helped me get loaded in to the front seat while huge snowflakes dusted our faces and clothing. Normally I would be giddy with happiness that it was snowing—and especially since it was coming down like big cotton balls—but this time I didn't care about it; I didn't care about anything.

We started driving down the road while the houses and buildings blurred past me. I felt guilty about holding my son in my arms, but what was the point of a car seat? What little time I had left I wanted to spend holding him.

We had been driving for ten minutes when we had to stop at a street light. There wasn't much traffic out on a Friday morning, but one car pulled up to the light and stopped on my right side. I felt uncomfortable, like I was being stared at, so I slowly turned my head toward the other car while we waited for the light to turn green. Then I realized why I felt the intense stare. A guy in his twenties was in the car next to us, with an empty car seat in the back of his car. He looked at me as though I was the most evil, horrible mother on the planet. He even went as far as to shake his head back and forth while expressing what could only be disgust.

It took me a few seconds to realize why he was looking at me this way, and when it hit me, I started sobbing uncontrollably.

"Chas, that guy thinks I'm a bad mom because I'm holding my baby in my arms instead of having him in a car seat!"

Chas looked mortified. He put his hand on my shoulder and caressed my arm. "Sweetheart, he doesn't know. Just don't look at him."

"You know how mad I get at parents who do the same thing—this just proves I *am* a bad mother!" I screamed. "I not only failed our son, now I can't even take care of his body right!"

"I'm sorry, honey. I'll drive on the right-hand side of the road so you don't have to deal with that. I should have thought of this—I'm so sorry," he said. His voice cracked with emotion and my heart broke even more.

I thought, *How much can the human heart take before it gives up and stops working?*

I continued to sob for a few miles and didn't look out my window any more after that. I kept my eyes on my precious cargo. His skin was starting to look a little darker and his cheeks weren't as full. I swallowed hard as I realized he wouldn't look like Connor for much longer. I had to soak in every moment until I had to let his little body go.

We stopped and picked up Chas's girls at their mom's house so they could spend a few days with us and attend the funeral. It was a somber moment. Usually when we pick them up, they come running out to greet us with "hello's" and hugs a-plenty. This time, they were packed, ready to go, and slowly got in their seats as they asked how I was doing.

Chas did his best to answer their questions, but the mood in the van was one of utter despair. It was as though the Grim Reaper had blanketed the entire vehicle with his cloak, and no one could penetrate the barrier it provided.

The rest of that evening is another blur. I do remember walking in our house, feeling like it was so empty. I took Connor to what was to be his room, gently touching his things, caressing his blankets and clothing, and even showed him the little stuffed animal his grandma had gotten him. "Little Toofers" was the stuffed animal's name—he was a baby blue dinosaur with cute little teeth sticking out. It was to be Connor's first snuggle toy.

My mom thought I was losing my mind. She called to tell me it was time to bring him to the funeral home, and that Connor had already seen all of his things. His spirit in Heaven was watching over us, and I was only holding his body—the host that had housed him until his time here was done.

I just couldn't process that Connor would not be spending any time in his crib, his room, his clothes—anything at all. It was too overwhelming. I sat down on my bed, holding my son's body, and just cried. I didn't know what else to do.

I was grateful for my beliefs and knowledge of our Savior, and I knew I would be with my son again someday, but reality was playing tricks on my mind. I just couldn't let go yet—I would never be able to. I would only learn how to deal with life differently.

Connor Charles Maddocks, infant son of Charles and Amy Maddocks, entered this world on December 31, 2006, and quietly returned to the loving arms of his Heavenly Father January 3, 2007. He was a strong little boy with a fighting spirit, who was nicknamed 'Spitfire' and 'Firecracker' by those who took care of him. Although his time with us here on earth was short, his effect on everyone was powerful and will last forever."

- Taken from the obituary written by Amy C. Maddocks -

Our precious baby boy came into this world a pound-and-a-half on New Year's Eve like a firecracker. His little body was perfectly formed and he could breathe on his own. His mom and dad and his six sisters rejoiced at the birth of their first little boy. But then he slipped quietly back into the arms of his Heavenly Father. His loved ones will miss him dearly. We are so grateful for the gospel that teaches us that the day will come when we can hold our beloved little boy once more.

- Anne Smart-Pearce, Connor's Grandma -

## CHAPTER NINETEEN

# A FUNERAL TOO SOON

The moment came when we had to bring Connor's body to the funeral home. The director had graciously waited at the mortuary until we were ready to arrive, so he ended up staying until around ten that night.

Chas, myself, and our five girls—Heather had gone back home to be with her husband—drove to the funeral home without one word spoken between us. A van full of seven people and nothing to talk about, bicker about, or even smile about.

We went in and met with the director, who was very kind and understanding. It turned out he knew more about me than I did about him—his wife was a teacher at the school where I taught. He let us take as much time as we needed while we all said goodbye to Connor, and then came the moment I had been dreading for some time; I had to hand over my son, knowing I would never get to hold him again.

My arms felt like lead. My feet felt like they were stepping through mud. The somberly lit room, with its delicate floral arrangements and lace doilies, felt like a trap. Every muscle in my body wanted to turn around, running, screaming, and protecting my son. Instead, I was cemented to the very spot I stood in.

Chas could see my inner turmoil. He asked the director if we could have a moment with just our family. He asked the girls to gather around, placed his hands underneath Connor while I still held him, bowed his head, and prayed.

It was the most beautiful, poignant, prayer I have ever heard. It gave me comfort and hope where I had none before. It gave me the strength to hand Connor to Chas and ask him to help me.

"Chas, will you give him to the director? I feel like I'm giving my son away, and I just can't do it."

He didn't need to respond. He gently took Connor from my aching arms. I kissed his little forehead and turned away. Alyssa held me while I sobbed, and Chas went into the other room to give our son to the director.

We all went to the van without talking, but with many tears. The ride home was too quiet, so Chas turned the radio on. Playing was a song by Phil Collins called, "You'll Be in My Heart." As I listened to the words, it gave me hope and strength to believe that I would see my son again—not as soon as I would have liked, but I would be with him again. Even though the lyrics weren't meant to signify death, they spoke to me on that level. They captured the thought of my love for Connor and how nothing would change that, not even passing away from this life.

After another sleepless night, we started making preparations for Connor's funeral. We had a meeting with the director, where we found out there was much to do. Graciously, the funeral home donated their services so the cost for a decent funeral wouldn't be a hindrance.

The biggest problem at that point was the obituary. In order to get it in the paper for the weekend, I had to have it to the funeral home by that afternoon. I had mere hours to write an obituary for my son.

Something took over inside of me. At the time I didn't recognize what it was—it would be months before I would. Yet as I was sitting there on a comfy couch, in an off-white room surrounded by beautiful furniture and decorations, I realized I didn't have time for self-pity. I took in my surroundings and felt at peace. I knew I could do this, and I had no other choice.

"Can you get me some paper and a pencil?" I asked the director.

He seemed confused, but composed himself and said, "Of course, I'll be right back."

"What are you doing, honey?" Chas asked me with that same confused look.

"I'm going to write Connor's obituary right now, so I don't have to worry about making a deadline this afternoon."

"Sweetheart, I don't think you are in the right frame of mind to do that."

I snapped, "When do you think I would ever be in the right frame of mind to write my child's obituary? This whole situation isn't right—there *is* no right time for this!"

I hadn't meant to sound so rude, but Chas understood exactly what I was saying.

I started working on it while helping Chas make other decisions. We both had tears in our eyes and our throats were dry from so much crying, but we got through it. We chose a casket, flowers, speakers, and even designed the program. Chas's mother is a very talented writer; words seem to flow from her so eloquently, you can imagine exactly what she's thinking when you read her work. She wrote a poem for Connor that was so beautiful we had to put it on the back of his funeral program.

### *Transplant from Our Garden to the Savior's*

We plant our gardens here on earth,
We give them tender care.
We lock intruders out,
But invite the Master there
And it is He who draws,
And masterminds the plan
That governs the birth and death of man,
He knows the very second we will die,
But often we can't accept and we cry,
"Oh, Father, do not take this precious little bud,
Let his petals unfold to maturity,
Choose from those grown old,
Please—let this little one stay yet awhile with me."
Beloved child, I know your pain,

It was given to me in Gethsemane.
It was not by accident I chose your son.
Have faith and lean on me.
I chose this perfect little one,
To make heaven more heavenly.
When they saw him coming, angels sang with glee,
And loved ones cried, "Oh, look who's here!
Oh Connor, Connor, Connor, dear."
When our tears of sorrow fall,
Their tears are tears of joy,
As loving arms reach out once more
To hold your little boy.
Just as you will again someday.
You'll watch him grow and laugh and play,
There is no doubt of this, you see,
For God is Love, and Love's for time,
And all eternity.

- Anne Smart-Pearce -

The poem spoke much to me, and I was so grateful to Connor's grandma for writing it, especially on such short notice. At the time I recognized it for its beauty, but I was so bitter.

Anger rose up inside me and seemed to consume my mind. I was mad at the world for what happened, including God, but even with all of this anger brewing, I was mostly mad at myself, that I had failed Connor.

That entire weekend seems a haze to me now, even more so than it did then, as if my mind has purposefully tried to block the negative feelings flowing through me.

We managed to get through planning our sons' viewing and funeral, putting together pictures and mementos for display, creating a funeral program with Connor's pictures on it, shaking hands and hugging hundreds of our family and friends giving their condolences, a long drive to the cemetery, and then a beautiful, but sad funeral.

Flowers, plants, cards, and meals poured in like a flood, invading every crevice. The community was just as shocked and almost as disappointed as we were, and they flocked to help.

Not knowing what else they could do, they brought comfort food. I was so grateful, because I wasn't able to stand for very long due to my incision, and I still had a family of seven to take care of. Meals continued for weeks as did the cards and condolences.

One of Chas's brothers offered to create a memorial Web site on which people could view pictures of little Connor and sign a guest book giving their thoughts. I had never heard of a memorial Web site and it sounded nice, so we gratefully accepted his offer. We chose the web address and he immediately got to work. Little did we know this would be the beginning of a little seed planted to help us on our road to recovery.

Two more Web sites would spring from that small beginning—www.connor-maddocks.memory-of.com and www.connor-maddocks.last-memories.com would also become healing gifts that sprung from the original.

Coming in with all of the cards and flowers were offers

to do service for us. I have never been one that can accept charity easily, and this whole experience shed a new light on that word for me. Chrysanne Henry, to whom I am forever grateful, is an amazing seamstress who owns a company called "See Our Creations," located in Hyrum, Utah. She is a friend of my mother's and remembers driving my daughter's bus to school when she was of elementary age. She called my mother and asked if there was anything she could do to help.

Of course we were all in shock, so she suggested making a beautiful blanket that had Connor's name, his sister's names, his birth date, stats, and other precious designs embroidered on it. She arranged to meet me at the fabric store to choose the fabric to use—a satiny baby blue, and she also made adorable little booties to cover his feet.

This action spurred a desire I had to make Connor's final resting outfit, so I also bought some white satin and spent part of the weekend making a gown for him with a little blue vest. On it I stitched six heart-shaped buttons—one for each of his sisters. He was so tiny, I had to buy a baby-doll outfit pattern and size it down. Thanks to Chrysanne's advice, it all turned out beautiful.

Monday morning, the day of Connor's funeral, a package arrived from Chrysanne. She had finished the exquisite blanket and booties, but also included embroidered handkerchiefs—one for each member of our family—with Connor's name, date of birth, and a picture of a lamb (the same one stitched on his blanket). She had tied all of these items in a beautiful package with a large white bow. At the bottom of the package was a framed poem she had written in 1997. It now hangs in my room. The words are timeless:

They're only on loan,
a gift from God,
these babies we call our own.
So we take them and love them,
the best we know how
and teach them until they're grown.
But some sweet spirits,
too precious and pure
will not need to stay very long.
And we never know
when the moment will come,
for Father to call
them home.

- Chrysanne Henry -

How do you repay such a kindness? How do you thank someone for helping to make a great loss like this a little less painful to bear? Sending a thank you card just didn't seem like enough, but I had time to do those things later. For the moment, all I could do was hold each item and treasure it for the short time I would have to enjoy it.

I sat down that morning and wrote a note to Connor. I asked Alyssa to run downstairs and copy it for me, and although she looked at me funny, she did as I asked, and brought me the copy and the original. I placed it in an envelope and sealed it, and then I wrote his name on the front. I would later place this note in his casket.

I also took a lock of my hair and cut it off, tied it with a baby blue ribbon, and prepared it for placement within his casket. At the time, I figured that it was a replacement for the lock of hair I was able to clip from him and keep with me. That way we would both have a piece of each other.

I was so busy preparing for the viewing that we arrived barely in time to dress Connor. Chas and I gently held him while dressing him in his clothes I had made. The booties were a little big, but we just giggled at that. I hadn't heard the sound of laughter in what seemed like ages, and it seemed out of place. We then laid him in his casket and let each of the girls place an object around him. Some of them drew a picture for him, and some gave him a stuffed animal or other memento.

A few moments later, the guests arrived. I could not believe the amount of people that showed up to pay their respects. There was a steady line for over two hours, and even at the end we had to move people quickly to finish up in time for the family prayer.

When my husband and the funeral director closed the casket, I couldn't bear to look. I had been strong while greeting all of the people, but I had to turn away during that time. With overbearing grief and sadness, I turned and looked for anyone to comfort me. I didn't care who it was, I just needed someone to hold me, and Chas was busy taking care of our son.

Heather, Chas's oldest daughter, saw me and embraced me as best she could. Alyssa and my father-in-law came over next, and the three of them held me while I sobbed. I knew I looked ridiculous, but I didn't care.

After the prayer, we slowly got into our cars and drove the twenty minutes to the cemetery. I felt as though I was still in a daze, dream-walking and not quite coherent.

Another beautiful service provided for us was the music at Connor's funeral. Our church youth group gathered there to sing a song of my choosing, "Nearer My God, to Thee," written by Sarah F. Adams, 1805-1848. This song was always my favorite church hymn, and I loved singing it. I had thought it appropriate for Connor's funeral, as my beliefs put him with God now that he had passed to the next life. However, I didn't realize this small act would ruin that song for me from then on. Every time I heard it after that—whether at church, on the radio, practiced on a piano—I always associated it with the death of my son and I always would.

The youth choir did an amazing job, and I am still so grateful to them for their strength. A few participants had a hard time getting through all of the verses, due to the overwhelming sadness blanketing us at the time, but others in the choir stepped up and filled in where it was necessary.

Many words were spoken to try and ease the sadness, but one particular speech was the most touching that day. Connor's grandma, Chas's mother, stood to recite a poem written by a dear relative that couldn't travel to be there that day. The poem reads as follows:

## *Father in His Wisdom Kept Me Near*

I heard his voice last evening say to me,
"My child, it is your time to go to earth,
You have been faithful through eternities,
You are prepared to know another birth."

And then I saw you mother, father dear,
I longed to be with you as once before,
But, Father in His wisdom drew me near,
"My child, you'll gain a body, nothing more,
And then return to live on Heaven's shore."
Where He leads me I will safely go,
In faith, that when you see Him, you will know,
Why, in His wisdom, He has kept me so.
For here, dear mother, father I am free,
I never will be sick or skin my knee,
Where all I know is love and good and right,
And here there is no darkness, only light.
Oh, mother, father dear, could you but see,
How Heavenly Father takes good care of me,
You will not mourn for long, nor shed a tear,
But walk in faith and knowledge, God is near.
And, if you will but true and faithful be,
Then, God will bring you safely home to me.

- Lynne Pearce Richards

Lynne told us in a letter, ". . . I don't profess to be a poet, but write from my heart. This was written for my own son who passed away at six weeks of age."

This poem spoke volumes to us. At the time, I just recognized it for its simplicity and beauty; later, I would come to agree with its words and profess the same. The congregation listened in silence as it was read out loud, giving the poem its due by listening intently and pondering the words therein.

The last person to speak at the funeral was our dear bishop. He spoke to give us words of hope, encouragement, and above all, faith. As I sat next to my husband, both of us shivering in the cold January evening, I realized this was it. The little coffin in front of me, with its beautiful spray of flowers, would be the last time I would be with my son until I met him again as I passed on.

I looked around at the other people in attendance, relatives who drove from far away, family who lived close by, neighbors, friends, co-workers, and even some of my students were all gathered around the small cemetery to be my strength. My daughters, surrounding Connor's casket, couldn't look up or meet anyone's eye. My mother, who had been with me through every medical emergency and decision along the way, looked at me through tear-coated eyes and tried to smile back at me. Even my father's side of the family, of whom I had not seen in years, were there to support me. I realized with horror that so many people were going to be affected by little Connor's death. *How could such a tiny little boy have such a profound effect on so many people?* I wondered to myself.

The ceremony was over and people were starting to move toward their cars. It was a cold January evening and getting colder by the minute. We had not had very much snow that winter, so we didn't have to fight trudging through snow, but now that the sun had set, it was getting colder very quickly.

I remember a few people hugging me, our girls putting their flowers on top of Connor's casket, and then I remember feeling totally and utterly alone. I could hear voices around me but I couldn't see any faces. I could smell the crispness of the fresh country winter air, but I could not enjoy it. I could even see the valley from the cemetery, as it was on the side of a mountain, but I couldn't revel in its beauty like I always did before. We picked this cemetery because I grew up in that city and had such fond memories of it. My grandpa was buried right next to Connor, and my uncle and aunt had graciously donated the burial plot to us.

However, all I saw, smelled, heard, and focused on was my little baby in his pretty white casket, laid before me with breathtakingly beautiful flowers. Nothing else surrounded me but an intense emptiness. My arms ached with a true physical pain to hold him. As if my Cesarean wound wasn't painful enough, the pain in my heart was inconsolable.

I suddenly realized everyone was leaving to go to the church and have dinner. Inside I panicked and made a decision that I was not going to leave my son alone, cold and lonely in a dark cemetery. I could see the cemetery sexton off to the side, trying to look inconspicuous as he spoke with the funeral assistants and directors. I knew he was there to lower my son's casket into the ground, to throw dirt on top of his body, and to cover the grave as though nothing was there. I truly despised that poor man, even though he was only doing his job which couldn't have been an easy one.

The world came crashing down on me then as though the atmosphere itself had decided to quit working and collapse to the ground. I fell to my knees before my son, placed my hands on his casket, and cried like I hadn't ever cried in my entire life. Sobs racked from deep within my body like an old lawn-mower motor trying to start, but having no luck. The pain and desperation was too much. I was not going to leave my son behind. *He should be with us! He should be in my arms so I can keep him warm!*

I don't know where Chas had been since the funeral had ended. His quiet strength left me after our bishop spoke as he mingled and took care of talking to people for me. But suddenly he was there again, by my side, holding me while on bended knee. He always seems to have a sixth sense about my moods and when I need him most. One of our favorite songs states, "You say it best when you say nothin' at all." It describes how we can feel each other's thoughts and moods without having to actually speak. He knew I needed him most at that moment, so he left whatever he was doing and rushed to my side.

"Sweetheart, it's time to go. We need to meet everyone at the church and it's getting dark."

"*No*! I won't leave him here—he's cold and it's dark and I can't leave him! I'm his mother and it's my job—my right—to take care of him!"

"Honey, he isn't here; you know this is just his body. His soul is with God now, happy and free from the pain he was suffering here. I promise you we'll come back here every day if you want to, but we really need to go now."

It amazed me how patient he was being with his delusional wife. But I still couldn't leave. My mother noticed what was going on, and came over to help. She and Chas finally convinced me to leave, with many promises of returning the next day, and they pulled me up from my kneeling position like a piece of taffy being removed from the machine that kneads it.

We stumbled toward the van together, Chas supporting my weight while my mother held the machine attached to my wound. When they had me in the car and she put the machine on my lap, I looked at it with disgust.

Fighting the urge to throw it off my lap, I said to Chas, "This isn't fair; I have to deal with the pain and wounds from delivering my son and I don't even have him with me to make it worth it. It was all for nothing."

"It wasn't for nothing, dear. You gave Connor a body, he lived when he shouldn't have been able to, and he stayed alive long enough that we got to know him and his fighting spirit. You should be proud of your wounds." Chas spoke quietly so the girls in the back seats couldn't hear him. "I'm jealous I don't have anything to show like you do. You will carry with you the scar of his delivery, always being a reminder that you gave him life. You should be proud, dear." I still cherish those words. How did he always manage to say just the right thing at just the right time?

We drove back to our neighborhood and went to our church. The Relief Society and compassionate service leaders from our ward prepared a feast for our family and loved ones. I mingled and thanked everyone I could get to, but I was so tired and in so much pain. I overheard a friend say to another as I passed by their table, "She is doing so well; I'm really surprised at how well she is holding up. You wouldn't know she just lost her only son."

Inside I snickered with disgust; if they only knew the truth, they wouldn't be saying such things. Or for that matter, if they had witnessed the scene I had just caused at the cemetery, they wouldn't feel that way.

In truth, I felt like a black hole had been formed in the middle of my heart, and it was slowly but surely sucking everything up around it to leave nothing behind. I had to fight to keep my sanity when all I really wanted to do was scream, yell, kick, fight, or otherwise throw a tantrum. I didn't even have it in me to be mad at the comment, implying I wasn't mourning my son *enough*. Either way, I was glad they didn't have to feel this kind of pain. I wouldn't wish it on my worst enemy.

To end the horrible day, we arrived home to find my stepchildren's mother waiting at the house to pick them up. Sitting there, with her smug attitude as she usually has, just added another thorn to my side. *Pour some more salt in the wound,* I thought to myself. *Twist the knife a little further.*

We all knew she was upset when she found out Connor was conceived—she did not hide that fact—so was she happy now? Lord knows she had caused me tremendous pain and stress during my pregnancy with her constant demands and the lawyer troubles she doled our way whenever she could. So was she personally gloating while waiting for us to return?

I would never know because I could never associate with someone who causes so many problems for people and seems to enjoy watching the pain and trouble it procures. I had given up many years ago trying to communicate with her.

I was sad to see the girls go, as they at least brought some life and energy to the house during this dreary time. But regardless, we said our goodbyes and waved as they drove away. I knew Chas' mood would be even more somber now, as it always is when he has to say goodbye to his girls and his visitation is over. He chooses not to show his children his sad emotions so they don't get upset and worry about him, but it wreaks havoc on our home because he is so depressed and melancholy when they leave.

With the mood one of dread, we all went to bed hoping against all odds that the morning would bring with it some semblance of normalcy. We were wrong; it would only get worse. It's always darkest before the dawn, and our beautiful dawn would have to wait some time before rearing its head.

*All day long I can hear people talking out loud,*
*but when you hold me near,*
*you drown out the crowd.*
*Try as I may I could never explain,*
*what I hear when you don't say a thing.*

*The smile on your face lets me know that you need me,*
*there's a truth in your eyes saying you'd never leave me,*
*a touch of your hand says*
*you'll catch me whenever I fall.*
*Yeah, you say it best, when you say nothin' at all.*

- Keith Whitley,

song lyrics from "Nothin' at all" -

CHAPTER TWENTY

# Now What?

That night, I didn't sleep. Chas had me take a sleeping pill after a few hours of tossing and turning, but even that couldn't penetrate the bitter cold I felt. I lay there thinking about my son. I would never see him smile, laugh, cry—nothing. My hopes were gone in what seemed like an instant.

When sleep finally did come, it was riddled with dream after dream replaying what happened in the hospital during that last week. Dreams and thoughts soon turned to nightmares as I relived the agonizing moments of Connor's death. Morning couldn't come soon enough.

Chas took the rest of the week off from work. He was grieving, but he also felt like he needed to take care of me. The home health care nurses came in every other day to change the dressings on my open wound, and meals poured in by the dozens, so my physical needs were being met. He was there to take care of my mental anguish.

Chas was like a rock in a rapid river that kept taking a beating but showed no signs of abuse. His pain was great, but he didn't show signs of it to those around him. Everyone that came to the door to offer their condolences, every delivery of flowers, plants, and food, he dealt with, and screened all the phone calls so I wouldn't be disturbed.

Alyssa was quite the trooper during this time as well. She acted grown-up in so many ways, taking my place around the house so I could wallow in my misery. She kept the house clean, fixed me plates of food to eat, helped Chas screen phone calls and visitors, and even kept accurate records of anyone that brought in any kind of plant, food, or card. She knew I would someday want to know who had helped out, but at the moment I didn't care.

I would lay in bed for hours pretending to be asleep, when in reality, all I was doing was staring at the ceiling or around the room. I hadn't gone in Connor's room yet; that door stayed shut for a while. I mostly thought about how pathetic I was. Millions of babies were brought into this world with worse circumstances than mine, and they *lived*. I had failed at what billions of women—for centuries—had succeeded at; with much less help. My pathetic excuse of a body couldn't even sustain life for my son for nine simple months.

One evening Chas and I were laying in bed watching the news on TV. He turned it off and rolled over to look at me. Then he asked, "Now what?"

"What do you mean—you just turned the TV off. Doesn't that mean you want to go to sleep?"

"No, I mean, what do we do with the rest of our lives? I thought our focus for the next twenty or so years was going to be raising our son. Now that he's gone, what are we supposed to do with the rest of our lives?"

Feeling shock and confusion at his words, I said, "I feel the same way. My every thought and focus since finding out I was pregnant was on what we were going to do, how we would raise our son, all the little moments we would have with him, and everything that has anything to do with being a parent. I have no idea what to say, think, or feel; let alone *do* with the rest of my life. I feel utterly helpless."

We talked for some time over the next few days about our feelings. Chas could focus on other things when necessary, but I wasn't able to do anything without somehow tying Connor's loss into it.

As if trying to deal with all of these horrible feelings wasn't bad enough, only two days after my son's funeral we were served with papers from a state agency Chas' ex-wife had contacted to see if child support could be increased. We were barely surviving on our current take home pay, and to have to give up even more would financially destroy us. Once Connor was born she wouldn't have been able to increase child support, but now that he was dead, she had free reign to have it recalculated. It was just too much to deal with. Now we had to deal with even more lawyers and paperwork, instead of being able to mourn the loss of our son.

Chas told me almost two years after Connor died that he felt like he never truly was able to deal with Connor's death, because he always had to deal with lawyers, courts, and problems his ex-wife caused. It wouldn't be until much later that he would be able to confront the feelings he had about losing his son.

Several days after the funeral, Chas finally forced me to go into town with him to get a few needed items for our home. I'm sure he hoped he could somehow "snap" me out of my constant state of misery, and maybe help me to stop hiding from the world. I reluctantly agreed.

While at the store, I was very limited by my movements. I still had the vacuum machine attached to me, and it hurt to move quickly. I stayed toward the front of the store where the books were while Chas and Alyssa did some grocery shopping. I was glancing through the books and magazines when I came upon a journal. Not putting too much thought into it, I added it to the basket I held. I then started looking through the different genres of books, trying to find something about losing a child. What kind of "genre" has to do with the loss of a child?

Not surprisingly, I didn't find anything. After all, I was in a grocery store—not a bookstore. But that sparked an idea. When I hooked up with Chas and Lys, I asked if we could stop by Borders or Deseret Book. They exchanged a funny look, but said we could. After they paid for the items, we started to drive to a bookstore, but realized we had to get home quickly because someone was bringing dinner (again). Funny thing about LDS women is, give them any kind of calamity, tragedy, or upset in life, and they cook. My church had gone above and beyond the call of charity in providing my family with enough food to feed an army for a month. We were so grateful; especially Chas and Lys. I couldn't move around real well in the kitchen yet, so they would have starved that first month had it not been for our neighbors and church members.

So the next day I had Chas drive me to a bookstore. I went to a local one in my area called, "The Book Table" and started investigating. I couldn't find what I was looking for, so I got very brave and went to the front counter. I thanked goodness it was an elderly lady working, because a snot-nosed teenager may have been less friendly and I wasn't in the mood to deal with anyone.

"Do you have any books on grieving?" I asked her.

"We do. If you were more specific I could guide you better, though."

I hesitated. This subject seemed so taboo. I wanted to turn around and go running out the door, but my limited physical capabilities prevented that, so I told her, "For the loss of a child."

"I'll show you where, sweetie," she said as she left her counter and guided me in the right direction. I knew in that moment that she *knew* what I was going through. *Had she lost a child, too?* I wondered. *How could she have known?* I didn't have the resolve to ask, so I just followed. She led me to an obscure corner of the building.

I looked around and thought, *So this is where they hide books on subjects nobody wants to talk about.* She showed me a little shelf I could look through, and told me to take as much time as necessary. So I did. I plopped myself and my wound machine down on the floor and starting reading.

It didn't take me too long; there weren't many, and I was disappointed at the slim pickings. But I eventually found two books and made my purchase. At the register, the woman asked, "Are these for you, honey?"

I thought to myself *What audacity,* as I lied and said, "No. They're for a friend."

She got a look on her face I would come to know quite well over the next little while; a look of pity. She knew I was lying, but I didn't feel it was any of her business.

"Well, I hope these help her feel better," she said, looking at me through sorrowful eyes.

I left the store and went home, but didn't pick the books up again until later that night. Instead, I found the journal I bought previously. It just sat there on my night stand, begging me to look inside. I could never have guessed the route my life would take at that point. A simple journal was all that was in front of me, yet that simple journal would change my life. The plain act of writing down my thoughts would alter everything I knew.

*I'm not ready to make nice,*
*I'm not ready to back down.*
*I'm still mad as Hell and I don't have time*
*to go round and round and round.*
*It's too late to make it right;*
*I probably wouldn't if I could.*
*'Cause I'm mad as Hell;*
*can't bring myself to do what it is you think I should.*
*I know you say can't you just can't get over it?*
*It turned my whole world around . . .*

- "Not Ready to Make Nice,"
by Dixie Chicks -

## CHAPTER TWENTY-ONE

# ENDLESS MONTHS

Late that night, one of many sleepless nights, I gave up on slumber and went to the kitchen to get a drink of milk. On my way to the refrigerator, the bag from the bookstore caught my eye. I poured myself some milk and sat down at the counter to investigate one of the books I bought. It was titled, "Gone Too Soon: The Life and Loss of Infants and Unborn Children," by Sherri Devashrayee Wittwer. I ended up reading through that ninety-seven page book three times in one night.

The next night, when sleep wouldn't come to me once again, I re-read the same book, only with pen and highlighter in hand. I wrote my thoughts in the margins and highlighted the points that particularly intrigued me. I continued this behavior several times over the next week, with that book and one titled, "Angel Children: Those Who Die before Accountability," by Mary V. Hill.

I also continued to write daily—if not hourly—in my journal. These acts helped me focus on the simple act of living. I found myself looking forward to reading and writing.

Even though sleep still evaded me, life was becoming bearable through my journey of discovery. *There were other women who felt like I did.* And yet, they were also speaking from a spiritual perspective, and at that point in my life, I had turned my back on God and anything to do with Him.

Nobody but my husband knew the anger and hatred I felt toward religion. I had not prayed to the Lord since the moment Connor died in my arms, and I was determined not to. God is omnipotent and can do anything, so why did He have to take away my precious son? I felt blasphemous and disrespectful, especially since so many people were doing so many things to help me in His name. Yet I just couldn't get over the fact that Connor didn't have to die, and even though my body failed him, God could have saved him.

At one point, many hours after Connor died, someone told me if I *really* wanted Connor to live, he could come back to life and stay with us. This man was a stranger, brought to talk to me by a dear family member. His words stung like alcohol being poured on an open wound. As if I hadn't prayed and wished for hours upon hours that Connor would live? To have someone actually suggest that I didn't love my son enough, or have faith enough to save him, was absolutely absurd.

I knew that all things happen for a reason, and nothing we can do will interfere with God's will, as He is all-knowing. Yet I could not fathom why Connor couldn't be alive. My bishop told us we would know shortly what Connor's purpose here on earth was, and it would bring us comfort and peace. I was too impatient to wait for that. I had to know right then why he was taken so soon. Yet through all of my reading, searching, pondering, and writing, no answers came. These acts gave me a purpose to keep breathing day-to-day, but they didn't answer the questions I had brewing inside of me.

I bought more books at larger bookstores, trying to make some sense of what I could do with the knowledge I gained. However, all the books I found only talked about the "stages of grief" and what I should expect during this time. I learned a lot about going through the shock, denial, anger, guilt, depression, confusion, and behaviors associated with loss. Yet this only confirmed that the feelings I was having were normal (if normal was possible at this point). I still yearned for something more and it wasn't coming into my life.

Weeks later my wound was finally starting to heal and I was able to change into "wet-to-dry" dressings. They taught my husband how to pack my wound with dressings soaked in a saline solution, and then put the same type of dressing—only dry—on top of the wet ones. This was supposed to act like a wick and when the wet transferred to the dry, it kept the wound clean so it could heal.

This was much easier than having to dope me up with Lortab pain pills, inject a deadening agent into and around my wound, rip the tape off, peel a spongy-type, stinky dressing out of the gap in my stomach, clean the wound with saline, measure and cut a new sponge to shove down inside the wound again, tape it back up, and hook it to my vacuum (every other day).

Needless to say, I was very grateful and relieved to get rid of the stupid machine I had been carrying around for what seemed like an eternity. I now had freedom of movement and my wound was feeling much better (or was it the pain pills I was taking several times a day?). I was starting to get around more, and I was even able to get on my computer and answer some emails that had come in from my substitute. That was one thing I never had to worry about—my job. The administration, teachers, and staff all took care of everything my sub needed while I was gone. Thankfully I had been prepared in advance for taking some time off, so my sub was able to see how I ran things based just off of my lesson plans—and go from there.

While on the computer, I remembered the Web site Chas's brother had spoken of. I went to it and cried for so long my eyes were puffy (nothing new, those days). He made a beautiful site in Connor's memory, including a guest book to sign, and he posted pictures Chas had either given him or he had taken from the funeral.

I also got curious and searched the words "loss of a child" on Google. Many sites came up, and I started looking around. After hours of searching and reading, I joined a forum for the M.I.S.S. Foundation, founded for families that have lost a child.

I stayed online the rest of that day, until Chas returned home from work. As I read through the questions and answers posted on the forum, I cried, laughed, and found a peace I hadn't had in some time. Finally—people who knew exactly what I was feeling. I posted an introduction of myself and waited for a response. Within ten minutes I had seven responses. Thirty minutes later, I had over twenty. The men and women on that site could see me crying out for help—by simply reading my introduction and telling about my little Connor.

Over the next few days I spent countless hours online reading, writing, posting, responding; all the while alienating my husband and daughter. I tried telling them about this new "group" I had found, and how they had made me feel so welcome. Lys thought I was a freak, but then again, everything I did lately was weird. She patiently told me to do whatever it was I needed to do in order to feel better, but later she told me she thought I was losing my mind.

Chas and I drifted further apart. All I wanted to talk about was Connor—all he wanted to do was get on with life. As he put it, we still had other children to think about. We couldn't keep all our focus on our dead son. I knew deep down he was right, but at the time I couldn't believe he would say such things to me.

I agreed I needed to get out and do more things, so the next time the girls came up to visit, we took them swimming at the local high school. I got in the water and swished around for a minute, then went to the side and watched the others. Chas was out in the middle of the pool playing catch with the girls and a soggy ball. They were laughing and playing, having a good time. So was everyone else in the pool. My world started to fog and swirl around me; I thought for a second I might faint. Instead, I started to cry. I turned toward the edge in hopes no one would notice, and after all, I was in a pool. Who would notice my puffy, red eyes?

Next thing I knew, Chas was behind me putting his hands on my shoulders and turning me around. Like I said, he seems to know when I am in need of him.

"What's going on, babe? Why are you crying?"

"I just can't believe all these people are having such a good time. How can they just play around like this when our son is dead?" I asked him, "How can I ever have fun, laugh, or enjoy myself when all I can think about is Connor and how he isn't with us?"

Chas looked at me with pity and concern. He tried talking to me about how we needed to enjoy life for Connor's sake.

"Honey, Connor is up there watching us. He is all around us, all the time—his spirit is surrounding us with love and adoration. Don't you want to make him proud? Don't you want him to see his mother making the best of her life?"

I confessed I still hadn't prayed to God since the moment Connor had died. Chas was shocked—I was always the strong one when it came to the gospel, yet he was picking up the slack lately for both of us. We talked for a few minutes about this line of reasoning, and I put on a happy face and told him to go play with the girls. I messed around in the water a few minutes, and then snuck out of the pool.

Back in the shower room I got cleaned up, dried off, and went to wait on the bleachers. I just couldn't have fun. I felt guilty for even wanting to try. I should be in mourning; not playing around at a swimming pool.

That was the beginning of my quest and determination to not have any type of fun in this life. I still went with Chas and the girls to movies, parks, theme parks, the mall, etc. But each time I was more and more distant. It was as if I was becoming a shell of my old self, just an apparition of what I used to be.

Also during this time, I started making scrapbooks and

putting together things of Connor's. I went to his room and started cleaning it out. Chas and Lys helped me move furniture around and carry things to storage. His room wasn't being used, and I finally realized it was stupid of me to keep it locked up.

I spent hours upon hours cutting and pasting. I also spent loads of money developing pictures. It was hard to believe that even though Connor only lived three days, we had taken hundreds of pictures of him. Oh, how grateful I was for those precious pictures.

I finally finished his scrapbook and showed it to everyone that came around. I showed them page after page as though everything was normal; as if I was showing off my son and his accomplishments. The scrapbook paled in comparison to the oversized one sitting next to it on the table; the one of Alyssa and her seventeen years of life. I still look at the two books of my children's lives and feel a twinge of heartache that one will always be so much larger than the other.

Chas bought me a corner curio cabinet to display Connor's things. I placed it in our room by my side of the bed. I also spent many hours rearranging the items I had collected: his foot-and hand-prints, molds of his hands and feet, a lock of hair, our hospital bands, his first set of clothes, and the blankets he snuggled in—the list went on and on. It's still proudly displayed as I add and continually rearrange it to suit my mood.

Throughout all the time I spent doing these things, my family worried that I was becoming obsessed. I probably was; but I didn't care. My actions were healing to me and brought me much needed peace. It was one of the few things I could do for my son. I realized how fearful I was of people forgetting about him. When I posted those fears on my online forum, I received numerous validations that this was common and normal. Every parent who has lost a child—at any age—lives in fear that their child will be forgotten. I was doing everything in my power to not have that happen.

I bought all kinds of trinkets with Connor's name on them. I bought stickers and decals declaring I had an "angel baby," and I even bought things so my family members could join in my madness. When I gave my mom a car sticker that said, "Proud Grandma of an Angel Baby," she looked at me as though she was going to cry. She comes from the old-school thought that you weren't supposed to talk about children that died, let alone announce it. I'll never forget that look. She truly believed I had lost my mind.

Then came another horrible day when I was woken up by a phone call from my mom, asking me, "Honey, are you okay?"

"What are you talking about Mom? I'm still in bed."

"Sweetheart, I saw the paper this morning, and your brothers did as well. We're all just really concerned with your behavior lately, and we want to help. What can we do for you?"

"What are you talking about? I have no idea what's in the paper, and what do you mean by my 'behavior'?"

"So you didn't put Connor's obituary in the paper again?" she asked.

"What? What do you mean? It's in the paper again? The same one?" I was appalled.

She told me to go get the paper and call her back. I went out to the mailbox and frantically turned to the obits. Sure enough, the very first obituary was my precious Connor. I read it word for word, even though I had it memorized. The only difference was that my grandpa's name had been added as preceding Connor in death. We had purposefully not put any of Connor's great-grandparents in the obituary because he had so many and we were limited on space by money.

I thought to myself, *who would do such a thing?* Surely there must be laws against this—could someone from the paper have done it? That didn't make any sense, yet here I was, looking at my son's picture in the paper once again. I decided to let it drop and deal with it later. I called my mom and explained to her I had most definitely not put that in the paper again. It brought all those painful memories I had worked so hard to cork, back to the surface. I hung up the phone and sobbed once again, all alone, with that longing ache in my arms to hold my son.

Later that morning, I turned on my computer and checked my email. My inbox had more than ten new messages, all from colleagues, friends, and neighbors, asking how I was doing. They had seen the obituary and thought I had lost my mind. To make it worse, they all believed I had done it to get more sympathy. The church leaders in my ward called to see if we needed more meals brought in.

Then the phone started ringing. I answered the first few but screened the rest. Everybody was calling to find out why I had put Connor's obituary in the paper again. I had to get to the bottom of who did it, so I called the newspaper.

After talking to several people, it was determined that a little old lady from the town where my grandpa used to live (and where Connor was buried) wanted the record set straight that he was related, so she paid to have it run again.

Needless to say, I was furious with the newspaper for allowing this to happen. I explained to them the pain I was suffering from seeing it again, not to mention all of the people that thought I was losing my mind. So they offered to print a correction.

The next day a few paragraphs were printed in the obituary section. The newspaper apologized for the mistake and confirmed it was not anyone in Connor's family that had requested it to be re-run. This stopped the calls and emails, but the damage was done. It had only confirmed in everybody's minds that I was loony.

To make matters worse, Chas and I were falling apart. He wouldn't let me talk about Connor anymore or show him the things I was buying or making. He wanted me to be *me* again—not this new person he didn't know. We got in fights and arguments that were stupid. We barely spoke to each other when we weren't mad at each other. I stopped doing things with him and the girls, and we grew further and further apart.

I mentioned these things on my forum, and it turns out this was "normal" too. Men and women deal with death differently—especially the loss of a child—and Chas and I looked like we were going to be just another statistic.

*I miss you.*
*Miss you so bad.*
*I don't forget you.*
*Oh it's so sad.*
*I hope you can hear me.*
*I remember it clearly.*
*The day you slipped away;*
*was the day I found it won't be the same . . .*
*I wish that I could see you again.*
*I know that I can't.*
*I hope you can hear me . . .*

- "THE DAY YOU SLIPPED AWAY,"
BY AVRIL LAVIGNE -

## CHAPTER TWENTY-TWO

# A LIGHT?

Time passed so slowly over the next month. I was feeling better physically, but mentally I felt like I was going downhill fast. I used to be such a happy-go-lucky person, and it was all I could do to smile—let alone laugh.

One Saturday when we had the girls, we decided to take them to a local roller skate park. We were standing in line waiting to pay when something caught my eye. I looked to my left, and sitting on a shelf by the wall was an upright stand holding little brochures. The picture on the pamphlet was of an adult hand holding a tiny premature infant with little tubes going through his nose. It was precious and tender. I walked over and picked one up. By that time, Chas had paid for the kids and they were ready to skate.

I went and found a comfortable table to sit down and read the paper I had picked up. It was an advertisement about the March of Dimes. I read through the entire brochure, educating myself about the foundation and their mission. I had heard of it as a child, and as an adult, any time someone came to my door I donated five or ten dollars, yet I never knew of their divine mission until now. I did not realize their sole purpose was to help premature infants and promote healthy pregnancies.

I felt a spark in the core of my soul that I hadn't felt since the day I had found out I was pregnant. It was tiny, but a spark nonetheless. The brochure talked about forming teams and getting donations. I thought, *Is this something I could do in Connor's memory?* I took a few brochures and decided to look into it.

For the first time in a long while, I watched the girls skating and smiled at their laughter. We stayed for a couple of hours while the kids played, had pizza and soda, and overall had a good time with each other.

Chas looked at me from across the table with love in his eyes, and it gave me some hope. Everyone kept telling me that with time, all things would be better, and maybe this was some small way it could happen.

When we got home I immediately got on the computer and went to the March of Dimes Web site. After reading for a while I decided I was going to form a family team and see who would support me. I would name it "Team Connor" and help to raise money for others, so maybe they wouldn't have to go through what I had to. I signed up online and immediately began working on the Web site they gave me to collect donations. I sent emails out to everyone in my address book, hoping they would donate. I poured myself into the project, and for a small time, it truly helped ease the pain I was suffering.

I knew time was healing my physical wounds, but it would

never heal my broken heart—it would only make it a little easier to deal with. The March of Dimes event was something I felt such passion for. I couldn't understand why, until talking with Chas about it. Later that evening we sat down and talked about what had been going on with our relationship lately. We both realized we were grieving differently about our loss, and we needed to come to an understanding of that.

All of our fights and arguments were the combination of the pent-up feelings we were having and not being able to have an outlet. I was making scrapbooks, Web sites, and putting together mementos of Connor, whereas Chas didn't want to see things that had to do with him because it hurt too much. He was trying to keep himself busy fixing things around the house or otherwise taking care of me, and I was pushing him to be a part of my grief in ways that just wouldn't work for him.

After talking about these things and realizing (finally) that men and women grieve differently, and coming to the conclusion that it was okay to do things differently, our marriage came to a point where we knew we would stay together and work to make it thrive. We believe we can be sealed together as a family in the Lord's holy temple, and that would allow us to be together forever. We determined that the temple would be our goal and we would do whatever was necessary to make sure it happened.

In several of the books I had read recently, I had come to the conclusion that I *would* be with Connor again, but I needed to be worthy to be his mother. The same went for Chas; we had to live a life of always striving for perfection—just like the

Savior had taught—so that when the time came, we could be with our son again and be proud of the life we had lived.

I realized the feelings I felt the evening I discovered the March of Dimes brochure came from my sweet Connor. For a brief moment I had felt the way I had when Connor was in my womb, and although I didn't recognize it at the time, I did now. Connor was trying to give me a message, and I wasn't going to disregard it.

I poured myself into trying to get team members to do the "walk" with me and to donate as much money as they could. Money was really tight for us at home because I had been out of work for almost two months. My school district approved me to take out of a "sick bank" leave pool where people donated some of their sick days to help out. This helped immensely, but didn't cover everything; especially with all of the medical bills and such that were now piling up.

I was in a bad frame of mind thinking about our financial woes when I received a special visit from a dear friend. A woman I taught with in a previous school came to see how I was doing. I had been avoiding her and many of my close friends, even though they were there for me through all of my trials.

My friends finally got fed up with me and just showed up when they knew I would be home—and otherwise couldn't turn them away. The moment I answered the door this time, I just sobbed in her arms. *Why had I been so against seeing her?* I needed my friends and I was pushing them away. It felt so good to show her all of Connor's belongings and to be able to talk freely about him and the things I was doing in his memory.

We spent quite some time talking and crying, and she had

brought with her many cards with personal notes from the staff at my old school. I read through each one as though they were special treasures. She patiently waited for me to finish, and then handed me one more envelope. In it was a check for a substantial amount of money, gathered by her from many generous people in my old school district. Everyone wanted to help in whatever way they could.

I was so overwhelmed with the love and sacrifice they had made for me. The money they collected would help our family tremendously. I felt so blessed to have such a generous gift from so many people. That was a turning point for me in regards to my relationship with the Lord. I knew I needed to thank Him for putting these people in my life.

Chas had been talking to me for some time about not blaming the Lord, and how I was never going to feel peace unless I was willing to pray to Him for guidance and gratitude. So after my friend left that day, I got down on my knees and prayed like I never prayed before. I begged forgiveness for blaming Him, for not being able to sustain little Connor's life a little bit longer, and for turning my back on the one person that I knew would be the only one to get me through this rough time. I asked for strength in fighting my demons, strengthening my marriage and family, and knowledge that my precious Connor was serving a more divine purpose than he could have here on earth.

That prayer was the longest, most heart-wrenching prayer I had uttered since I had begged for Connor's life to be spared. It was spiritually cleansing in a way not possible before. After I finished, I felt calmness spread over me like a blanket, and I knew that although I still had difficult times ahead of me, I was going to get through this. I also knew I could never turn my back on the Lord again. He was my peace, my sanctuary, and the one person who would always be there for me, even when I had rejected Him.

Just like my dear husband had been telling me all along, I finally realized I needed the Lord in my life more than anyone or anything else. From that moment forward, I would seek always to communicate with the Lord, knowing He was my only salvation.

The next day, Lys drove me to the store for a while just to get some fresh air. I had a really hard time being in public places, so she took me to a small store where there weren't a lot people. As we walked in, I tried convincing myself I would be just fine. As soon as my feet crossed the threshold of the building, I felt a weight crash down on me. Everything around me looked perfectly normal; bright lights showing the groceries, captivating signs pointing to sale prices and good deals, people busily pushing their carts around, and yet there was something different. As I looked at the people, it seemed like every other person was pregnant or had a baby in their cart.

*How is this possible?* I asked myself. *This many people couldn't be at this point in their lives at this exact minute, could they?*

As Lys got a cart and put my purse in it, I stopped in my tracks. I couldn't bear to step one more foot closer to all of these people. My mind screamed that I was a freak and there was no reason for me to not go grocery shopping, yet my subconscious told me that all of the public was out to get me. How could I have such conflicting emotions at one time?

Lys turned to look at me and knew something wasn't right.

"Mom, what's wrong?"

"I can't do this, honey. I need to go home," I told her.

"Mother, it's the grocery store. I know you don't like being around a ton of people right now, but it's just a small store. Surely you can handle walking around a few people. Don't be ridiculous."

"You don't understand, Lys. I don't know what's wrong with me anymore than you do! I am a 'people' person and always have been—you know that. But everywhere I look, someone is enjoying the moments and experiences I should be having right now, and it's tearing me up inside. I can't explain this to you, and I don't expect you to understand, but I just can't do this," I said.

She wasn't accepting my response—at all. She simply turned around while telling me I was going to follow her or she'd push me in a wheelchair, but either way, she was going to make me go shopping.

I reluctantly followed her. I felt like I was in a tunnel being led down a murky corridor to my doom. Every person that stepped into my peripheral vision had a baby or small child. I kept my eyes away from them as much as possible, but sometimes I couldn't avoid them. I started noticing their children and would inwardly cringe whenever I noticed it was a little boy, yet when I saw a little girl, all I did was notice how cute or adorable she was.

This realization cut me deeply. I knew it would always hurt to look at baby boys, and at the rate I was going, I was destined to run into every mother in the valley that had a newborn son. Underneath my insanity, my mind kept repeating over and over, *It's okay, you can do this, just a few more minutes, keep it together.* Yet outwardly, I'm sure I looked like a little girl with her eyes full of tears just waiting to pour over the side of her eyelashes.

There was no way Alyssa could know what torment my mind was putting my body through. I wanted to appear normal, and I knew Lys was worried about me, so I continued putting one foot in front of the other while she finished the shopping list. I knew if I opened my mouth I would burst out crying, so I pursed my lips together and followed her around.

After what seemed like an hour—but was actually only ten minutes—we were finally finished. I asked Lys if I could go to the car while she checked out (realizing I was acting like a child asking her mommy), and then started to make my way to the car. I put my head down and walked as fast as my injuries would allow me.

This would be the first of many anxiety attacks while I was in public, but at the moment, I was only worried about getting to the peace and comfort of my home. I made it to the car and quickly closed the door like I was shutting evil out with it. How could these people act like nothing was going on? *How could they be so "normal?" Didn't they realize people like me were losing their children every day?* These thoughts and others ransacked my mind like a fountain overflowing with water—I couldn'tkeep them from tumbling out.

Underneath it all I knew I was being ridiculous, but I wasn't rational at the moment, and it frightened me to realize my mind wasn't the same anymore. Like a child being afraid of the dark, I suddenly felt the world pushing in on me. Gravity was ten times its force at that moment; pushing me further into the seat of the car. I wrapped my arms around my empty abdomen, somehow hoping to fill the gaping hole my son had left behind when he left this world. I sat there with tears rolling down my face, waiting for Alyssa to come back.

By the time she returned with the groceries, I had composed myself enough to put a smile on my face. I couldn't hide my blotchy, swollen eyes, but she was used to that.

"Sorry sweetie. I didn't mean to freak out like that—I don't know what's wrong with me. I just can't seem to control my emotions."

"It's okay Mom. I know what's wrong with you—your son died and things will never be the same again. It sucks, but there isn't anything you can do about it. I just hope you will figure out how to deal with it better as time goes by."

I felt so utterly selfish at that point. I wasn't the only one suffering—Alyssa had lost a brother. It was unfair of me to wallow in my misery while everyone around me was suffering, too. Lys was acting like the adult; I like the child. Our roles had been reversed, but I wouldn't let it stay that way. I knew I would have to do something to pull myself together and deal with life. What kind of life that would be I didn't know, but I would not allow this tragedy to ruin my relationships with my loved ones still on earth.

We traveled the short distance home and started to unload the groceries. I could feel the peace surrounding my home like a bubble wrapped around it. When we walked up to the front door, there was an envelope wedged between the door and the jamb.

We went in the house and opened it. To our surprise, it was a check of donations a colleague from my school had collected from everybody. I had only been teaching there a year, and most of that had been spent in the hospital. I was again overwhelmed with gratitude. These dear people had donated so much we would be okay financially for a couple of months. I couldn't believe their sacrifice for someone they barely knew. And yet, it was believable—because the Lord was making this happen. Little Connor had touched more than just our lives; he had touched all that knew us. He had given others the opportunity to serve and give back to someone. This would be the beginning of many miracles to come.

*In this universe nothing is ever wholly lost.*
*That which is excellent remains*
*forever a part of this universe.*
*Human hearts are dust.*
*But the love which moves the human heart,*
*abides to bless the last generation.*

- Ralph Waldo Emerson -

## CHAPTER TWENTY-THREE

# GRATITUDE

As the days passed into weeks after the passing of my son, I fell into a pattern that would not prove well for me, nor would it for anyone. Realizing I could not sleep without having nightmares about Connor, I started taking heavy doses of sleeping pills. On nights I took my precious little blue pills, I was dead to the world. I would sleep for eight to ten hours a night and not remember a thing. My family would talk to me once in a while during these times and have conversations with me; but I wouldn't remember anything.

They started telling me I was addicted to the pills, but I argued with them, insisting that my doctor had told me they were not addictive. He had said they could be habit-forming, but not addictive. To me, that meant they were safe.

To prove their point, one morning Alyssa asked me, "Mom, what's the magic number?"

I asked, "What are you talking about?"

"You know; the magic number we agreed on last night. The one you said you would remember and would tell me what it was in the morning," she said.

"Chas, do you know what she's talking about?" I asked him, as he stood close by.

"Yes, every night about twenty minutes after you take your pills, you seem to be still awake, but in the morning, you never remember what we talked about." he said. "We give you little tests, like 'remember the magic number' and you don't."

"Good grief! Well, at least you all get a laugh out of my stupidity," I told them.

We giggled about it for a bit, then the subject changed to something else and it was forgotten. But it wasn't really forgotten; I could tell by the looks in their eyes they were concerned. All I knew was that I was finally getting some much-needed sleep and my nights weren't filled with the ever-present horror of knowing my son was dead. It never occurred to me I was becoming dependent on the pills. Not necessarily "addicted," but definitely needy. I put off the inevitable and went about trying to make some sense of my life.

Anything I could do that made Connor's life "real" to me—and everyone else—was taking over my every waking moment. I continued scrapbooking all of the hundreds of pictures we had taken; both of his life and death. I worked diligently on creating not one but two Web sites in his memory. I created keepsake boxes, shadowboxes, domed glass containers full of "angel" relics and Connor mementos, everything that had anything to do with him. Every time someone came to the house to visit or bring something over, I would drag them into my room to show them the curio full of Connor's relics. I was so proud of it—acting as though I was showing off my son's accomplishments. While these things were helpful to me, they were also becoming an obsession.

I still had a hard time in public and had to force myself to go out. I spent a lot of time in the tub, trying to soak away my pain and sorrow. I spent countless hours holding Little Toofers, Connor's stuffed toy. It seemed to be the only thing I could wrap my arms around to try and push away some of the bareness I felt between my arms where my child should have been.

A few weeks after Connor's death, I made a goal to go back to church. All the kids were with us and we purposefully walked into sacrament meeting late so I wouldn't have to talk to anyone while we filed in the chapel. We sat down and I tried to make myself busy by reading the hymn book. After the program started, I stole a few glances around me. With sudden horror I realized I was surrounded by pregnant women and babies—*how could the Lord do this to me!* I screamed in my mind.

I fought off hyperventilation, and tried with all my might to stop the water about to pour over the edges of my eyelids. They were pooling deeper and I knew I couldn't hold it much longer—the dam of tears was going to break no matter what I did. Luckily, I had tissues with me and just kept dabbing and wiping, hoping against all hope nobody would notice me.

It must have worked for a while, because not even my husband noticed for at least ten minutes. When he finally did, he put his arm around me protectively and asked what was wrong.

I whispered to him, "Honey, every woman here is either pregnant or has a little baby in their arms. It's like I'm being punished!"

He must have been choosing his words carefully then, because after a few seconds of pausing, he whispered back to me, in all seriousness, "Sweetheart, did you really think we were the only ones who have sex?"

I looked at him as though he'd lost his mind, saw the smirk in his smile and twinkle in his eyes, and burst out giggling. His wife was making a fool of herself crying in church, and he was making jokes. Of course, his ruse worked; it made me laugh enough that I was able to stop the tears and focus on what was being said by the speaker—instead of all the women and babies.

I wasn't brave enough to fight the crowd, though, and left a few minutes before the closing prayer. Chas was able to deal with the questions and comments for me while I hid in the car. It would take a few more tries before I could sit though all of church and deal with the sympathy and questions. But Chas was with me every time, helping me by making me laugh whenever I got too serious.

Once I made the mistake of sitting on the back row of my Sunday school class. Apparently, this section was reserved for parents with little children. I couldn't focus on the lesson because of all the little babies and toddlers surrounding me with their cuteness.

*Am I being punished again?* I thought.

One toddler was being especially bratty; disobeying his parents, making messes, running around all crazy, and his mother had a hard time trying to control him. I could only smile and wish I had those problems. That young mother had no clue how lucky and blessed she was.

When her son got more vocal, the mother picked him up, looked at me apologetically, and asked me, "Do you want a baby? I'd give him up right now for free."

In all reality, how many times have we heard something or said something similar to that—only in jest—but still, just the same?

All I could do at that moment was cry. I turned my head into my husband's chest and cried. He held me close until I had myself under control and then we walked out.

The woman looked at me like I was a freak. She didn't associate my strange behavior with her comment; she must have thought I was just "having problems."

I wanted to scream at her—and the world, *Do you think I wanted to be a part of this club? Do you really believe I enjoy being a bereaved parent?* I never asked to be a part of this. My entire being had changed completely. I was no longer the same person I was before my son died. My personality, my attitude, my demeanor—everything had changed. There was "me" before Connor died, and now there was "me" after Connor died. I felt like two different people inhabiting the same body.

Sometimes tidbits of my old self shine through, and for brief moments, life feels "sane" again, and normal. But those moments are few and far between, like a flickering firefly on a cold summer's night. I feel as though I grasp for my old identity like a toddler trying to pick up a toothpick—I know it's there, it's just always a little out of reach. I often wonder if my two identities could ever meet and call a truce.

People starting commenting on how "well" I was doing; the buzz through the neighborhood was that I was coping so well, it was remarkable. Even my extended family started believing I was going to be my old "self" soon. However, they didn't see what went on behind closed doors, when no one else was around. When Lys and Chas were at school and work, the house was empty except for me and the gaping hole in my spirit, and I didn't have to put up pretenses. These were the times when I was most vulnerable. I think I called my mother at least five times a day—and for thirty minutes or more each time.

Whenever I was working on something that had anything to do with Connor, I was fine. Yet I still had to take sleeping pills at night and pain pills during the day for my wound. Whenever someone saw me in public, I talked and laughed as if everything was normal. But when I was alone, I felt as if the walls were slowly shrinking in on top of me and I felt like screaming—many times I did.

The days and weeks started turning into months, and before long I was able to physically return to work. Mentally, I was scared beyond my wits. It wasn't like I had a job where I could go and work and keep to myself. I was a teacher. I had to put on a "happy" face every second of the school day and function at a level I hadn't been at for months.

When I went back, my co-workers made the transition much more bearable than it should have been. They welcomed me back with open arms, offered assistance whenever it was needed, and gave me the space I needed. My students were understanding and glad to have me back. I fell into the routine, like putting on your favorite pair of jeans you haven't seen for months—it just felt right.

At the end of each school day I was physically and emotionally exhausted, and most days I would lock my classroom door after the final bell rang, trudge over to my desk, and collapse in my chair while trying to control my sobs. *Why was grief so exhausting?* Even though I was teaching and putting on a happy face for everyone, inside I felt so empty and alone. *How long will this last?* I mused. Even though everyone was trying so hard to make me feel comfortable, nothing was truly the same. A few teachers asked me about Connor, and even let me talk about him. Some would hear the subject and leave the area quicker than you could say "taboo." Others would cry with me and hold me while I wept like a little girl. Still others didn't know quite what to do with me; they would stammer and stutter while trying to ask me how I was doing.

This behavior transferred over into the public arena as well. Pregnant women who knew me avoided me like a sickly rat. People thought if they associated with me or got close to me, they could somehow "catch" whatever it was that had killed my son. I was like a walking "baby killer virus" that was avoided at all costs. I would even see women in my church on Sunday walking down the hall toward me with their swollen bellies and turn the other direction while looking down and avoiding eye contact.

I would come to realize later (much later) that they just

didn't know how to deal with me. They didn't know what to say. What do you say to someone who has lost their child? Nothing ever said is going to make things right—but something said lets you know someone cares.

I allowed myself to feel slightly accomplished when I could go to a crowded place like a community event and not have a panic attack, or could say Connor's name without choking up, or if I could simply get out of bed one morning and not resent the fact that I was still alive.

It was then I realized I needed something else—everything I was doing just wasn't filling this hole Connor had left me with. I tried pouring myself into volunteer work. I searched online for opportunities, continued my work with the March of Dimes, and looked for opportunities to assist in my local community. I learned that whenever I kept myself busy—I didn't have time to focus on how sad I really was.

My doctor put me on anti-depressants. This was a *most* disturbing moment for me, for I have never been one to believe in using pills for mental problems. I had always been so strong in my personality and attitude, and had always believed ninety percent of people on pills for mental stress just needed to "buck up" and deal with life. Yet when Dr. Nordell decided I wasn't dealing with things like I should be, he ordered me to take the pills *and* see a shrink. Me, the mentally strong one, take pills and talk to a quack? *How could I have let myself get to this point?* I wondered.

There was no getting around it once my husband got wind of the doctor's orders—he made sure I did both. I felt a little better when a psychologist told me I simply had "situational depression." Apparently this was much better than "clinical depression" because it would go away with time, acceptance, and counseling. I only saw the psychologist a few times, and I really did enjoy the visits I had with him. It was nice to be able to talk so freely with someone I knew wouldn't judge me or avoid me because I had lost a child. I also would have liked to continue seeing a counselor, but I felt uncomfortable because I thought I needed to deal with my problems, and I shouldn't have to talk to someone else to straighten me out. So I quit seeing the counselor after a few visits.

I spent a lot of time—no, a lot is an understatement—hoards of time on the Internet. I poured over reading material, focus groups, forums, and blogs, anything that could help me feel "normal" again. The M.I.S.S. Foundation forums became my favorite. I gained many new friends from that support group, ones that even now I still depend on.

I started realizing the only time I felt truly at peace was when I was serving others. I got more involved in church service projects, helped at community events, and even started working with a non-profit organization called the Angel Teddy Bear Foundation. They were formed with the purpose of providing teddy bears and support to parents so they will not have to go home from the hospital empty-armed. I volunteered making sure all the local and major state hospitals were supplied with the teddy bears and documentation needed to help grieving families.

Spring was finally here, and so I decided to try and volunteer again with a local heritage center. My daughters and I had volunteered there each summer as living history interpreters at an 1860's pioneer site, and it was work we loved. The farm was having their "Baby Animal Days" event, where the community gets to come and pet all the new life at the farm. My family had always worked with the baby chicks, so that's where we were placed again.

One challenge we always faced was keeping the chicks safe from harm. We have to continually rotate them so they don't get too handled, and we were doing a good job.

Then it happened—a young boy was too rough with one of the chicks and it stopped moving. I quickly picked it up and started walking away with it, trying to see if it was okay. Its breathing was labored and I could tell it was slowly dying. I ran to the edge of the trees, away from people, and broke down sobbing.

Alyssa and Chas came over and tried to help. I sat down and held the chick up to them, "Please don't let him die!"

Alyssa whispered to Chas, "Why is she so upset? This happens all the time."

Chas replied, "Think about it, Alyssa. She just lost her baby son, this chick is also a baby."

At least he seemed to understand me. I didn't realize I was associating the two events until I overheard him saying that.

I had to go home after that, as I couldn't focus on anything but that poor baby chick. I didn't see an end in sight to my upsetting emotions. I felt like a swiftly flowing river, careening down a mountainside out of control—when would I be able to stop and relax again?

Later that month, I went to my first Share meeting. Share is an organization of parents and health care professionals working together to provide support toward positive resolution of grief experienced at the time of, or following, the death of a baby. Usually they visit you in the hospital and help you take care of your baby, but I didn't receive this benefit because I had been flown to a different hospital to have Connor, so there was no one to talk to me when he died. Instead, I found out about the group from my sister-in-law (who is a nurse at the local hospital), and after wrestling with myself about going to a "support" group for a couple of months, I finally caved to my emotions and went.

Chas wouldn't go with me, as he was uncomfortable with talking about Connor's death at that point. So I braved it myself. I walked down the hallways of the hospital, feeling like they were closing in on me. I followed the signs pointing to "Share Parents Meeting" and found the open door down a long corridor. I hesitated outside the room, trying to decide whether I should back out or go in.

Then someone noticed me and said, "Hi there, come on in. What's your name?"

"Hi. Is this Share Parents?"

"Yes, it is. Come in and sit down, We'll be starting in a few minutes,"

I found a seat in the room, toward the back, hoping no one would notice me. Funny thing is—everyone in that room kept their eyes down. Nobody looked around and noticed each other. I realized what I was doing, why I was there, and what we were going to talk about. This brought the tears freely. They started pouring down my cheeks while I tried in vain to keep my eyes dry. Nobody said anything to me—they just went about their time setting up the room, situating things, talking to friends—not once saying anything to me. At the time, I thought this was strange behavior; *shouldn't someone be asking me what's wrong?*

Then my brain kicked in—duh—everyone was here for the same reason. We had all lost a child. Nobody needed to ask me what was wrong, because they all knew. Suddenly I felt better about being there. The lights seemed to get brighter, the walls opened up, and I felt peace come over me. Of course, that didn't stop the tears, but I did feel better inside.

The meeting started and each person in the room introduced themselves and told the others about their loss. I wondered, *Was this what AA meetings were like?* Leave it to my ever-funny mind to make a joke out of a sad situation. You could call that a "coping mechanism." Or you could say I was losing my mind. Either way, it made me giggle inside.

My turn to share came, and share I did. I was amazed at how freely I told about my miracle pregnancy, birth, and the tragic death of my sweet Connor. Here I was, in a room full of strangers, and I was talking openly about what had happened. All ten people in that room watched me with concern in their eyes as I finished. All ten of those people knew exactly how I felt. All ten of those people actually cared about me and what I had gone through. And all ten of those people had no clue who I was—they took me in and graciously accepted me as part of the "group" because they all *knew*. We now all belonged to this "club" nobody wanted to be a part of, but we were all grateful to have.

I left the meeting that night feeling like angels were carrying me out the door. I wouldn't describe it as a weight being lifted off my shoulders, but more of a space being filled in my hole of sorrows. A tiny space, but a space, nonetheless.

I thanked the Lord that night for all I had been given. I still felt bitter and empty about my son's death, but I was grateful for the situations and people He brought into my life. I started to see a small light at the end of my tunnel of grief.

*No act of kindness,*
*no matter how small,*
*is ever wasted.*

- Aesop, "The Lion and the Mouse" -

*Let your light so shine before me,*
*that they may see your good works,*
*and glorify your Father*
*which is in heaven.*

- Matthew 5: 16 -

## CHAPTER TWENTY-FOUR

# AN EPIPHANY OF SORTS

One afternoon I was on my way home from school and had to stop at a friend's house to deliver some items she needed. She led me into the office of her home and we sat down to chat. As we talked about our current situations in life, she felt inspired to give me a book to read. The book was by Richard Paul Evans entitled *The Five Lessons a Millionaire Taught Me about Life and Wealth.*

I left that day thinking, *Why this book—how can this possibly apply to me?* I couldn't see the correlation, so I put the book in the back of my car and went home. It sat around on the corner of my kitchen cupboard for a few weeks until my friend sent me an email asking me if I had read it. I felt guilty, especially since she had felt so strongly about giving it to me, so I found it under a stack of papers on a table and sat down to read it.

It was a quick read—first, it was short; second, it was entertaining; and third, it spoke to me on a level I never knew I had. The correlation between this book and my loss of Connor was not obvious; in fact, it didn't strike me until half way through the book.

I learned many things from that book, and continue to learn from it still, but at the time, these major points stood out:

Money isn't evil like most people are taught.

I deserved to have sufficient for my needs and my family.

I had to be wealthy in order to "give back" to others.

In his book, Mr. Evans states, "We end where we began. Life is not about money. It's about God. It's about love. It's about family and relationships. In sharing with you these principles, it is my hope that you will always give back, that you might find life's true abundance."

This little book sparked a desire within me that still burns to this day. It planted a seed of aspiration that continues to grow. I immediately started putting the principles taught in the book into use. I wanted to be financially stable to the point that I could give back to the world in Connor's memory and honor.

I had always believed that those who are "rich" must be greedy and dishonest. Sure, I always wanted a piece of that money pie, but I didn't know how to get there without falling into the trap of greed. Mr. Evans gave me the hope I needed to do what I needed to do, to not only take care of my family but also to make Connor proud.

I started thinking about my financial situation and realized how much good I could really do in the world if only I had the means to do it. It's true that money doesn't buy happiness, but it does buy security and hopefulness. If used correctly, like the Lord intended, it can offer charity beyond belief.

When it was time for the March of Dimes walk, I was proud

of the meager amount I had collected, but I would have been so happy to give more of my own money. Any and every donation goes to good use, but imagine if organizations like it all around the world had more funding available. Maybe, just maybe, Connor would have survived if there had been funding for more research.

I decided that everything I could do to help prevent another mother from having to go through what I did—I would do. I poured myself into doing all I could for others. Every time I did something to help someone else, I felt like my little Connor was watching me, holding me, comforting my soul, and being immensely proud of me.

I knew that if I couldn't be with Connor at this time on earth, the least I could do was to make him proud of me until we could be together again. So I worked myself ragged trying to help wherever I could.

Chas tried being gentle with me, like I was a petal of a delicate flower being tossed around in a whirlwind.

"Honey, you really need to slow down. You aren't going to physically heal completely if you continue working this hard. You have to still take care of yourself."

"I know, dear. I'm fine. Can't you see I have to do these things in order to keep my sanity? I will truly lose my mind if I slow down," I replied.

"But sweetie, do you really think Connor is going to be proud of you if you work yourself into an early grave? No, he wouldn't. You need to focus on yourself, too."

"I know, I know. I just hate to stop and focus on the sadness. When I'm helping others, I focus on how happy I was when Connor was here. Yet when I'm doing nothing or doing something for myself, I start to focus on the misery and the gaping hole in my heart," I told him.

"Well, you need to find a balance between the two. I'm not trying to upset you; I'm just worried about you. And remember, you still have living family members to take care of. Connor is being administered to by angels—we need you here," he quietly said.

He had been trying so hard to not upset me; choosing his words so carefully, speaking in a soft voice, and holding me. I knew he was right—I couldn't shun my living family for my dead one. I decided right then I would do whatever I could to find that balance.

The realization that Connor is constantly watching over us and working hard in the after-life until we meet him made me want to do everything in my power to be the best person I could be.

I made up my mind to behave as if Connor were in the room with me—because I believe he is—as I believe all our loved ones from beyond the veil are. If there is one main uniting factor that bereaved family members feel, I believe it is the common faith we share that our loved ones are waiting for us on the other side. Regardless of race, gender, religion, or any other category society places upon us, the death of someone close to us—especially a child—brings with it the hope, faith, and realization that there is an afterlife. Our world does not end with death; it is merely the next chapter in the story of our amazing existence. A bereaved parent would have a hard time functioning without this knowledge, and so the survival mechanism in us all kicks in and the Lord lets us know our children are waiting for us, perfect and whole and complete. We *will* be with them again and it will be in a realm where peace reigns supreme and love abounds.

I began looking for all kinds of opportunities to do good deeds. It is amazing how many you can find surrounding you every day. Flyers and posters started catching my eye for community events that needed sponsors and volunteers, newspaper announcements stood out that were announcing items where people needed support, radio ads screamed to me from the airwaves about times and places where I could help others. I scoured all the resources I could find in order to plan accordingly. I also recruited my family, friends, and even church members to join me in my quest to make the world a better place.

Most of my "mental" support group willingly volunteered their time, and those who couldn't, donated money for the causes I was supporting. One event at that time really joined my family and community together. We participated in a major feat of building a community park completely by volunteers and donations. A little boy had died when he was around two years old, and his parents, having experienced the same outpouring of kindness from those around them as we did, decided to give back to the community and memorialize their son by building a park in his name. The entire community rallied together to build that park—our family included—and we worked countless hours sawing, hammering, and putting together a safe, fun place for the public to enjoy.

Imagine for a moment, actually close your eyes and paint a picture in your mind, of what the world around us would be like if everybody on this planet did one, simple, random act of kindness each and every day. Seriously, think of what our world would be like. When you give a little of yourself to others, there is an automatic feeling of pure love and joy. Serving others generates an aura of contentment. Your actions may seem so small and insignificant and yet, if *everyone* did something with a loving heart, our world around us would change. And it would change *rapidly*. People wouldn't have the time or desire to hold grudges or do ill to others. It is truly amazing to envision what our world would be like if all of its inhabitants would strive to do kindness to others.

It's amazing to realize that all this change, all these good works, all this charity and love for our fellow man, came because of one tiny little boy. His existence changed the lives of multitudes of people. I believe the world is a better place because of my son, due to the lives he changed just by being here for three short days. I'm not saying life is perfect—it won't be perfect until we are with our children once again. There are many days when I am mad at the world because my little Connor is not with us right now—especially when I see parents who neglect their children. Something as simple as not covering tiny legs with a blanket when it's cold outside will get my blood pressure rocketing. But for each of those "angry" times, there are precious untold moments of "happy" times when I remind myself that my life is worthwhile and precious. And I need to live my life in such a way that when I do return to Connor, my grandpa, my father, and all my loved ones that have gone before me, I will be able to stand before them with pride, knowing I did all

I could on this earth to make life a little easier and worthwhile for those around me.

A parent who has lost a child at any age is a changed person. People quite often say, "You are doing so well! It's like you are back to your old self again." In reality, a bereaved parent will never be their "old self" again. What others may see on the outside is simply a false image of what is really going on within you. A part of your heart died with your child.

I think and believe the missing piece of our hearts is in safe keeping with our loved ones who have gone beyond the veil. When we are reunited, they will fill that abyss we now have. We will once again be whole and complete—one with ourselves and with them.

I feel it is our responsibility and our *privilege* to do random acts of kindness and charitable acts for others, in memory of our dearly loved children, preparing the way for when we join them in paradise. Connor and all our babies did not die in vain—their legacy lives on in how we treat and take care of others.

Connor had a purpose on this earth and I will not let that purpose be forgotten. He brought together many people who now go out of their way to help others in this world. I believe there is good in all of us but sometimes it takes one special spirit to help us find that good and use it as it should be—in the service of others.

What is truly most amazing is that all this became true for me, my family, and my community because of one little boy who was just too precious for this earth.

*Some are born great, some achieve greatness,*
*and some have greatness thrust upon them.*

- William Shakespeare -

CHAPTER TWENTY-FIVE

# FINAL THOUGHTS

The following phrases are what I call my "Amy-isms." Too often in life, we take the shorter path to get somewhere quicker. Whether traveling to your job, your home, or even on vacations, we often don't take the time to truly enjoy life. Over time I have taught myself to live by these rules—Connor taught me to live by these rules. We need to stop and realize that not only is our time on this earth short, it can be easily wasted away by living too quickly. This is our only chance, our one shot, and we don't get a repeat. We don't get the option of rewinding or starting over. I say, make the very best of your every moment. Don't waste your precious, precious time. When I live my life this way, I imagine doing these things with Connor. I imagine him watching me from above, being proud of me, excited for the day when we will be together.

I live each and every moment with the intent that someday I will look back on my life and know that I lived it well. I don't want to have regrets. I never want to say, *If only I had more time, I would have done things differently.*

When I actively participate in doing the "little" things, I know I am doing all I can to live well, to make Connor proud of me, and to prepare myself for the time when I will be with my son again. These may seem corny to some, weird to others, or downright stupid to many, but to me—they are necessary. Make your own list and stick to it. Your life and the lives around you will be better for it.

Run through the sprinklers
Go barefoot
Make every moment count
Turn off the TV
Play games
Take it easy
Indulge your senses
Put up your feet
Breathe deeply
Kick back
Build sand castles
Break with routine
Laugh often
Feel good
Smell the ocean
Have a picnic
Make someone's day

Appreciate the little things
Take the scenic route
Visit nature
Be happy
Live with intention
Savor the moment
Sleep under the stars
Have adventures
Go places
Go out and play
Plant flowers
Be spontaneous
Do it for the fun of it
Enjoy life
Skip rocks
Feel the sun
Eat outdoors
Let your spirits soar
Share stories
Try new recipes
Cherish family
Settle for more
Delight your friends
Dance like you are the only one around
Sing as though nothing else matters
Love like getting hurt doesn't matter
Chocolate is worthless, without caramel
in it or on it (just my opinion)

In conclusion, I would like to add a list of things a bereaved parent can choose to do to remember their children and help them grieve, as this is necessary. I am so grateful to the staff at the hospital where I delivered my son, to Share Parents, and to the countless women and men online that all gave me their support and ideas for mementos and keepsakes to keep my son's memory alive. I share these ideas with you now in the hope that you will find peace and contentment in the things you do for your children, family and community.

- Keep a journal—either of your days, or written personally to your child.
- Scrapbook pictures of your pregnancy and any pictures you have of your child. It's *your* choice how you display this scrapbook.
- If possible, have molds made of your child's hands and feet.
- Display items in a curio, shadowbox, or memory box. Items could include molds, pictures, locks of hair, hospital bands, pregnancy tests, anything that touched your child, intended gifts, or anything at all that reminds you of your precious one. I like to collect Willow Tree figurines of mothers and their children and anything that has something to do with angels.
- Have "angel pics" taken of your child if they were stillborn or died while an infant. There are some companies who will even do this service for free (see Web sites).

- Create Web sites in memory of your child.
- Create new holiday traditions. My favorite is what I call "Connor's Kindness Gifts." My friends and family do random acts of kindness for strangers and we collect them to put in a specially made stocking for my son, then on his birthday, New Year's Eve, we read them out loud to see all the kindness done in Connor's memory.
- Save everything that had anything to do with your child. You may want to display them or keep them in a special place for you and loved ones to go through at certain times throughout the year. I have both—some items I display year round; others I keep for just myself and my husband.
- Plant trees or a flower garden in memory of your child.
- Donate an outfit, blanket, or other item a child may need to your local hospital—especially on important days like your child's birthday, angelversary (death date), or holidays.
- Create new holiday memories that include your child—they are with you in spirit. I buy an ornament each year for Christmas with the year printed on it and make it appropriate for the age Connor would be.

Remember that anything you do is what is right for you—don't let others dictate what you should or should not do. Only a bereaved parent truly knows how you feel and, even then, everyone has a different outlook and situation, so only *you* truly know yourself.

The following list was given to me by a dear friend when Connor died and it speaks volumes about how a bereaved parent feels. It was written by an organization called Compassionate Friends.

## *Bereaved Parents' Wish List*

1. I wish my child hadn't died. I wish I had him back.
2. I wish you wouldn't be afraid to speak my child's name. My child lived and was very important to me. I need to hear that he was important to you also.
3. If I cry and get emotional when you talk about my child, I wish you knew that it isn't because you have hurt me. My child's death is the cause of my tears. You have talked about my child and you have allowed me to share my grief. I thank you for both.
4. I wish you wouldn't "kill" my child again by removing his pictures, artwork, or other remembrances from your home.
5. Being a bereaved parent is not contagious so I wish you wouldn't shy away from me. I need you now more than ever.
6. I need diversions so I do want to hear about you; but I also want you to hear about me. I might be sad and I might cry, but I wish you would let me talk about my child, my favorite topic of the day.

7. I know that you think of and pray for me often. I also know that my child's death pains you, too. I wish you would let me know those things through a phone call, a card or note, or a real big hug.
8. I wish you wouldn't expect my grief to be over in six months. These first months are traumatic for me, but I wish you could understand that my grief will never be over. I will suffer the death of my child until the day I die.
9. I am working very hard on my recovery, but I wish you could understand that I will never fully recover. I will always miss my child, and I will always grieve that he is dead.
10. I wish you wouldn't expect me "not to think about it" or to "be happy." Neither will happen for a very long time, so don't frustrate yourself.
11. I don't want to have a "pity party," but I do wish you would let me grieve. I must hurt before I can heal.
12. I wish you understood how my life has shattered. I know it is miserable for you to be around me when I'm feeling miserable. Please be as patient with me as I am with you.
13. When I say "I'm doing okay," I wish you could understand that I don't "feel" okay and that I struggle daily.
14. I wish you knew that all of the grief reactions I'm having are very normal. Depression, anger, hopelessness, and overwhelming sadness are all to be expected. So please excuse me when I'm quiet and withdrawn or irritable and cranky.

15. Your advice to "take one day at a time" is excellent advice. However, a day is too much and too fast for me right now. I wish you could understand that I'm doing good to handle an hour at a time.
16. Please excuse me if I seem rude, it's certainly not my intent. Sometimes the world around me goes too fast and I need to get off. When I walk away, I wish you would let me find a quiet place to spend time alone.
17. I wish you understood that grief changes people. When my child died, a big part of me died with him. I am not the same person I was before my child died and I will never be that person again.
18. I wish very much that you could understand; understand my loss and my grief, my silence and my tears, my void and my pain. But I pray daily that you will never understand.

Along with this list are words of advice for those who mourn.

## *The Mourner's Bill of Rights*

Allan Wolfiet, PhD

Though you should reach out to others as you do the work of mourning, you should not feel obligated to accept the unhelpful responses you may receive from some people. You are the one who is grieving and, as such, you have certain "rights" no one should try to take away from you. The following list is intended both to empower you to heal and to decide how others can and cannot help. This is not to discourage you from reaching out to others for help, but rather to assist you in distinguishing useful responses from hurtful ones.

1. YOU HAVE THE RIGHT TO EXPERIENCE YOUR OWN UNIQUE GRIEF.
   No one else will grieve in exactly the same way you do. So when you turn to others for help, don't allow them to tell what you should or should not be feeling.

2. YOU HAVE THE RIGHT TO TALK ABOUT YOUR GRIEF.
   Talking about your grief will help you heal. Seek out others who will allow you to talk as much as you want, as often as you want, about your grief. If at times you don't feel like talking, you also have the right to be silent.

3. YOU HAVE THE RIGHT TO FEEL A MULTITUDE OF EMOTIONS.
   Confusion, disorientation, fear, guilt and relief are just a few of the emotions you might feel as part of your grief journey. Others may try to tell you that feeling angry, for example, is wrong. Don't take these judgmental responses to heart. Instead, find listeners who will accept your feelings without condition.

4. YOU HAVE THE RIGHT TO BE TOLERANT OF YOUR PHYSICAL AND EMOTIONAL LIMITS.
   Your feelings of loss and sadness will probably leave you feeling fatigued. Respect what your body and mind are telling you. Get daily rest. Eat balanced meals. And don't allow others to push you into doing things you don't feel ready to do.

5. YOU HAVE THE RIGHT TO EXPERIENCE "GRIEFBURSTS."
   Sometimes, out of nowhere, a powerful surge of grief may overcome you. This can be frightening but is normal and natural. Find someone who understands and will let you talk it out.

6. YOU HAVE THE RIGHT TO MAKE USE OF RITUAL.
   The funeral ritual does more than acknowledge the death of someone loved. It helps provide you with the support of caring people. More importantly, the funeral is a way for you to mourn. If others tell you the funeral or other healing rituals such as these are silly or unnecessary, don't listen.

7. YOU HAVE THE RIGHT TO EMBRACE YOUR SPIRITUALITY.
   If faith is a part of your life, express it in ways that seem appropriate to you. Allow yourself to be around people who understand and support your religious beliefs. If you feel angry at God, find someone to talk with who won't be critical of your feelings of hurt and abandonment.

8. YOU HAVE THE RIGHT TO SEARCH FOR MEANING.
   You may find yourself asking, "Why did he or she die? Why this way? Why now?" Some of your questions may have answers, but some may not. And watch out for the clichéd responses some people may give you. Comments like, "It was God's will," or "Think of what you have to be thankful for," are not helpful and you do not have to accept them.

9. YOU HAVE THE RIGHT TO TREASURE YOUR MEMORIES.
   Memories are one of the best legacies that exist after the death of someone loved. You will always remember. Instead of ignoring your memories, find others with whom you can share them.

10. YOU HAVE THE RIGHT TO MOVE TOWARD YOUR GRIEF AND HEAL.
    Reconciling your grief will not happen quickly. Remember, grief is a process, not an event. Be patient and tolerant with yourself and avoid people who are impatient and intolerant with you. Neither you nor those around you must forget that the death of someone loved changes your life forever.

## WEB SITES

### Connor's Web sites

www.connor-maddocks.memory-of.com
www.connor-maddocks.last-memories.com

### Support

The M.I.S.S. Foundation, www.missfoundation.org
Share Parents, www.nationalshareoffice.com
Mommies Enduring Neonatal Death, www.mend.org
The Compassionate Friends, www.compassionatefriends.org
Angel Teddy Bear Foundation, www.angelteddybears.org
Bereaved Parents of the USA, www.bereavedparentsusa.org
Precious Memorials, www.preciousmemorials.com
Journey of Hearts, www.journeyofhearts.org
Baby Loss, www.babyloss.com

### In Memory Of

Memory Of Web sites, www.memory-of.com
Last Memories Web sites, www.last-memories.com
Angel Pictures, www.babyangelpics.com
Sympathy Tree, www.sympathytree.com
Unending Legacy, www.unendinglegacy.com

### Others

Remembering our Babies, www.October15th.com
www.nowilaymedowntosleep.org
Digital Scrapbooking, www.designerdigitals.com
www.mycanvas.com
www.picaboo.com
March of Dimes, www.marchofdimes.com

**Memorial Days**

National Children's Memorial Day—The second Sunday in December

Pregnancy and Infant Loss Memorial Day—October 15th

**A Few of My Favorite Healing Books**

*Gone Too Soon: The Life and Loss of Infants and Unborn Children*
by Sherri Devashrayee Wittwer

*Angel Children: Those Who Die Before Accountability*
by Mary V. Hill

*Help, Comfort & Hope after Losing Your Baby*
by Hannah Lothrop

*Small and Simple Things*
by Marjorie Pay Hinckley

*The Five Lessons a Millionaire Taught Me about Life and Wealth*
by Richard Paul Evans

*The Christmas Box*
by Richard Paul Evans

*The Life Beyond*
by Robert L. Millet & Joseph Fielding McConkie

*Empty Cradle, Broken Heart: Surviving the Death of Your Baby*
by Deborah L. Davis

*My Three Wishes: Be Your Own Genie*
by Bretton K. Hadfield

*The Secret*
by Rhonda Byrne

*You never said "I'm leaving."*
*You never said, "Goodbye."*
*You were gone before I knew it,*
*And only God knows why.*
*A million times I've needed you,*
*A million times I've cried.*
*If love alone could've saved you,*
*You never would have died.*
*In life I loved you dearly,*
*In death I love you still.*
*In my heart you hold a special place,*
*No one can ever fill.*
*It broke my heart to lose you,*
*But you didn't go alone,*
*For part of me went with you,*
*The day God called you home.*

- Author Unknown -

## CHAPTER TWENTY-SEVEN

# POETRY

The following poems got me through some of the roughest nights after my son died, and while sometimes they made me cry, other times they made me smile. I know there are many, many poems that speak to your heart. These spoke to mine and I hope you may find peace and comfort in reading them.

# *If I Could Have a Lifetime Wish*

If I could have a lifetime wish
a dream that would come true
I'd pray to God with all my heart
for yesterday and you.
A thousand words can't bring you back
I know because I've tried
and neither will a million tears
I know because I've cried.
You left behind my broken heart
and happy memories too
I never wanted memories...
I only wanted you.

- Unknown -

# *Do Not Stand by My Grave and Weep*

Do not stand by my grave and weep.
I am not there. I do not sleep.
I am a thousand winds that blow.
I am the diamond glints on snow.
I am the sunlight on ripened grain.
I am the gentle autumn rain.

When you awaken in the morning hush,
I am the swift uplifting rush
of quiet birds in circled flight.
I am the stars that shine in the night.
Do not stand at my grave and cry.
I am not there, I did not die.

- Mary E. Frye -

# *A Father's Grief*

It must be very difficult
To be a man in grief,
Since "men don't cry"
and "men are strong"
No tears can bring relief.

It must be very difficult
To stand up to the test,
And field the calls and visitors
So she can get some rest.

They always ask if she's all right
And what she's going through.
But seldom do they take his hand,
"My friend, but how are you?"

He hears her crying in the night
And thinks his heart will break.
He dries her tears and comforts her,
But "stays strong" for her sake.

It must be very difficult
To start each day anew.
And try to be so very brave-
He lost his baby too.

- Eileen Knight Hagemeister -

# *Remembering*

Go ahead and mention my child,
The one that died, you know.
Don't worry about hurting me further.
The depth of my pain doesn't show.
Don't worry about making me cry.
I'm already crying inside.
Help me to heal by releasing
the tears that I try to hide.
I'm hurt when you just keep silent,
Pretending he didn't exist.
I'd rather you mention my child,
Knowing that he has been missed.
You asked me how I am doing.
I say "pretty good" or "fine."
But healing is something ongoing,
I feel it will take a lifetime.

- Elizabeth Dent -

# *Father in His Wisdom Kept Me Near*

I heard his voice last evening say to me,
"My child, it is your time to go to earth,
You have been faithful through eternities,
You are prepared to know another birth."
And then I saw you mother, father dear,
I longed to be with you as once before,
But, Father in His wisdom drew me near,
"My child, you'll gain a body, nothing more,
And then return to live on Heaven's shore."
Where He leads me I will safely go,
In faith, that when you see Him, you will know,
Why, in His wisdom, He has kept me so.
For here, dear mother, father I am free,
I never will be sick or skin my knee,
Where all I know is love and good and right,
And here there is no darkness, only light.
Oh, mother, father dear, could you but see,
How Heavenly Father takes good care of me,
You will not mourn for long, nor shed a tear,
But walk in faith and knowledge, God is near.
And, if you will but true and faithful be,
Then, God will bring you safely home to me.

- Lynne Pearce Richards -

# *A Walk to Remember*

I walk to remember the steps you'll never take
I carry you with me as I firmly plant my feet
Our trek started long ago, before my belly swelled
You were a love that grew, like butterfly wings that beat
Your gentle flutters then become kicks
upon which I would dwell
And I would talk to you, sweet babe,
about the world you soon would meet
The sun always shone down upon us then,
when you were in my womb
And I eager to show you the world
that would have been your home
How you'd have loved the sun shining,
blue skies without a cloud
The autumn leaves turning, the snow falling all around
The flowers in the summer
would have filled your eyes with smiles
And the rain that might have fallen
would have caused your great surprise
You would have traveled far with me, holding me by the hand
And I'd have shown you all I could, more than I can imagine
You hold my heart tightly now, as though we're holding hands
How far we've traveled, little one,
and my life with you has been sweet
For I carry you in my heart as I firmly plant my feet

- Kathie Mayo -

# *Letter from Heaven*

To my dearest family, some things I'd like to say.
But first of all, to let you know, that I arrived okay.
I'm writing this from heaven. Here I dwell with God above.
Here, there are no more tears of sadness;
here is just eternal love.
Please do not be unhappy just because I'm out of sight.
Remember that I am with you
every morning, noon and night.
That day I had to leave you
when my life on earth was through.
God picked me up and hugged me and
He said, "I welcome you.
It's good to have you back again;
you were missed while you were gone.
As for your dearest family, they'll be here later on.
I need you here badly; you're part of my plan.
There's so much that we have to do, to help our mortal man."
God gave me a list of things that he wished for me to do.
And foremost on the list, was to watch and care for you.
And when you lie in bed at night
the day's chores put to flight.
God and I are closest to you . . . in the middle of the night.
When you think of my life on earth,
and all those could have been loving years.
Because you are only human,
they are bound to bring you tears.

But do not be afraid to cry: it does relieve the pain.
Remember there would be no flowers,
unless there was some rain.
I wish that I could tell you all that God has planned.
If I were to tell you, you wouldn't understand.
But one thing is for certain, though my life on earth is o'er.
I'm closer to you now, than I ever was before.
There are many rocky roads ahead of you
and many hills to climb;
But together we can do it by taking one day at a time.
It was always my philosophy and I'd like it for you too;
That as you give unto the world, the world will give to you.
If you can help somebody who's in sorrow and pain;
Then you can say to God at night . . . "My day was not in vain."
And now I am contented . . . that my life was worthwhile.
Knowing as I passed along the way I made somebody smile.
So if you meet somebody who is sad and feeling low;
Just lend a hand to pick him up, as on your way you go.
When you're walking down the street
and you've got me on your mind;
I'm walking in your footsteps only half a step behind.
And when it's time for you to go . . . from that body to be free.
Remember you're not going . . . you're coming here to me.
And I will always love you from that land way up above,
Will be in touch again soon.
P.S. God sends his love.

- Ruth Ann Mahaffey -

## *To Those Who Look Away*

To those who look away when I grow teary-eyed
in the baby department: look a little deeper.
Surely you have some compassion in your heart.

To those who change the subject
when I speak my sons' names,
change your way of thinking.
It just might change your whole life.

To those who roll their eyes
and say that we barely had them at all,
how could we miss them so much?
In our hearts we have seen them live a thousand times.
We have seen their first steps, first day of school,
their weddings, and their children.
We have had them forever in our minds.

To those who say we can have another, we did.
I thank God for her everyday,
but even if I have twenty more babies,
I will forever have two in the grave—
and that is two too many.

To those who say to get on with my life,
I have. It is a different life,
The life of a grieving mother.
One with a tremendous amount to be thankful for,
but also one with a lot to mourn the loss of.

Do not judge the bereaved mother.
She comes in many forms.
She is breathing, but she is dying.
She may look young, but inside she has become ancient.
She smiles, but her heart sobs.
She walks, she talks, she cooks, she cleans, she works;
she IS, but she IS NOT, all at once.
She is here, but part of her is elsewhere for eternity.
Do not dismiss us:
we have shaped more than just the future generation.
We have released all the tiny angels
who are watching over you.
Open your eyes to US
and you just might see THEM.

- Unknown -

# *Just Say I'm Sorry*

You don't know how I feel; please don't tell me that you do.
There's just one way to know—have you lost a child too?
"You'll have another child"—must I hear this every day?
Can I get another mother, too, if mine should pass away?

Don't say it was "God's will"—not the God I know.
Would God, on purpose, break my heart,
then watch as my tears flow?
"You have an angel in heaven—a precious child above."
But tell me, to whom here on earth shall I give this love?

"Aren't you better yet?" Is that what I heard you say?
No! A part of my heart aches and I'll always feel some pain.
You think that silence is kind, but it hurts me even more.
I want to talk about my child
who has gone through death's door.

Don't say these things to me, although you do mean well.
They do not take my pain away; I must go through this hell.
I will get better, slow but sure—and it helps to have you near.
But a simple "I'm sorry you lost your child"
is all I need to hear.

- Gail Fasolo -

# *The Mention of His Name*

The mention of my child's name
May bring tears to my eyes,
But it never fails to bring
Music to my ears.
If you are really my friend,
Let me hear the beautiful music of his name.
It soothes my broken heart
And sings to my soul.

- Unknown -

# *Men Do Cry*

I heard quite often "men don't cry,"
though no one ever told me why.
So when I fell and skinned a knee,
no one came by to comfort me.

And when some bully-boy at school
would pull a prank so mean and cruel,
I'd quickly learn to turn and quip,
"It doesn't hurt," and bite my lip.

So as I grew to reasoned years,
I learned to stifle any tears.
Though "be a big boy" it began,
quite soon I learned to "be a man."

And I could play that stoic role
while storm and tempest wracked my soul,
No pain or setback, could there be
could wrest one single tear from me.

Then one long night, I stood nearby
and helplessly watched my son die.
And quickly found, to my surprise,
that all that tearless talk was lies.

And still I cry, and have no shame.
I cannot play that "big boy" game.
And openly, without remorse,
I let my sorrow take its course.

So those of you who can't abide
a man you've seen, who's often cried,
reach out to him with all your heart
as one whose life's been torn apart.

For men DO cry when they can see
their loss of immortality.
And tears will come in endless streams
when mindless fate destroys their dreams.

- Ken Falk -

# *Live for Me*

If I could, I would tell you that I love you,
And that I chose to spend the time I had with you.
If I could, I would tell you that you are not to blame—
For all was written in the stars, so long ago . . .

If I could I would tell you that I love you,
And just how much our time together meant to me—
How I remember every kiss, and the loving arms that held me
And in my memory, I'd beg of you, please don't forget to live!

LIVE FOR ME!
Don't take a moment for granted—
Every breath you take and every friend you make
is a precious, precious gift—
LIVE FOR ME!
Open up your heart and let the people that surround you
Help you love again—LOVE and LIVE for me!

If I could, I would tell you that I love you,
And I remember every precious moment shared—
I would ask you to release, any pain that still remains
And fill your heart with peace and love for you and me

If I could, I would tell you that I love you,
I would hold your hand and tell you that I'm fine.
'Cause here I play with the angels,
and I even dance with God (or among the stars)
And the love and light I feel is all I need!
LIVE FOR ME!
Don't take a moment for granted—
Every breath you take and every friend you make
is a precious, precious gift -
LIVE FOR ME!
Open up your heart and let the people that surround you
Help you love again—LOVE and LIVE for me!!!

Forgive yourself and love yourself and
Love all those around you—in memory of me—
LIVE FOR ME!
Your life is a gift of mine as much as it is yours—
So please, please, LIVE and LOVE for Me!

- Written and sung by the musical group, The Jajas -

*You fill up my senses*
*Like a night in the forest*
*Like a mountain in spring time*
*Like a walk in the rain*
*Like a storm in the desert*
*Like a sleepy blue ocean*
*You fill up my senses*
*Come fill me again*

- "Annie's Song" by John Denver -

# Acknowledgements

First and foremost, I would like to thank my Father in Heaven. Without the Lord, I truly would have lost my mind by this point in my life. His hand has been in everything I have done, including the bittersweet labor of love this book has been for me. There were many times when all I could write was one sentence—stopping to wipe my tears away as I relived moments dear to me. It has truly been a work of my heart, and although it was healing and fulfilling to write, the words would not have come if the Lord had not prompted me and allowed the words to flow from my mind. Truly the Lord's hand is present in all things.

I would also like to acknowledge my sweet husband; my rock, my saving grace, my pillar of strength. Words cannot express my love for this man and all he has done for me. I am so proud our son carries his name. His strength lifts me up when I need it, and his gentle ways allow me to freely guide myself and be independent when I need "Amy" time. He is a tall, mean-looking man who at first glance looks like he could tear your head off, yet he is really a big "teddy bear." He is truly a gentle giant. He loves to serve others and feels happiest when he can do so. He is also an amazing father who would do anything for his children, and I am so grateful our son has such an incredible dad. He calls me his "sweet Amy" and I know I am not always deserving of this title. Thank you, dear, for you, and for loving me the way you do.

Also I want to thank my sweetie, Alyssa. You are truly my sunshine. The angels broke the mold for perfect daughters when you came to this earth. Alyssa is one of the most determined, intellectual, adorable, loving, and precious daughters a mother could ever want. She is like a rainbow bursting through the dreary clouds, a tunnel of light at the end of a deep and dark cave, or a snuggly blanket to keep you warm. Thank you, Alyssa, for allowing me to be your mother and for acknowledging and being proud that you have a little brother in heaven.

If I were to acknowledge everyone that has helped me, guided me, supported me, and made a difference in my life, I would have to write another book to include them all. My family and friends know how much they mean to me. In particular, I need to thank my mother. She lost a grandchild and had to suffer that loss as well as suffering through her daughter's pain. She supported me through all my trials and gave me the courage I needed to continue telling my story and getting it on paper. Thanks for always allowing me to cry on your shoulder or for letting me laugh out loud, Mom. I love you!

And a special thanks to my dear sister-in-law, Marie, who lets me go on and on and on about my precious Connor—wherever and whenever I need to. She allows me to talk about my son as though he is here with us and recognizes that I sometimes just need to cry, laugh, or scream.

The same goes for my sister, Katie. She patiently listens to me as I complain about not having my son here on earth and we cry together some days over missing our father. Thank you, Katie, for always being able to make me smile. Your aura lights up a room!

Because of the following people in my life, I am a better person—thanks to them for helping me get Connor's story told and for their help and support: Karen Christoffersen—a true angel on earth; Richard Paul Evans—an inspiration to all and a fabulous mentor; Robert Allen—an amazing motivator and mentor; and to the WriteWise program for helping to craft who I am as an author.

Thank you to all those men and women out there who take the time to listen to bereaved parents and let us talk about our children. We truly are better people for having you in our lives and hopefully we can someday repay the favor by "paying it forward."

Lastly, thank you for reading this book and allowing me to share Connor's story with you. I had to leave out so much that happened, but I hope I was able to show you a glimpse of what my family, friends, and community went through as we all experienced the loss of my son. I also pray that this book will help spread the message that there are bereaved parents all around us every day, and if you will just allow us to keep our children's memories alive, the world will be a better place for it. And for those of you who read my book that have experienced the loss of a child, I hope my story, advice, and words of hope will bring you much needed peace.

- Amy C. Maddocks

# About the Author

Amy C. Maddocks lives in the beautiful mountain valley of Cache County, Utah, with her husband and children. She received a Bachelor's degree in Education from Utah State University and currently teaches language arts.

Amy and others are dedicated to promoting doing good toward others and building self-esteem. She is a volunteer with many organizations, both online and in her local community, and enjoys doing presentations about the loss of children and how families and communities can cope with such a loss while making a wonderful life in memory of the child who passed away.

Amy has many other books in the beginning stages that are inspirational and motivating. Visit www.amymaddocks.com for more information or to arrange for a speaking engagement.